THE
UTURN
CHURCH

NEW DIRECTION
FOR HEALTH AND GROWTH

THE U TURN CHURCH

NEW DIRECTION
FOR HEALTH AND GROWTH

KEVIN G. HARNEY & BOB BOUWER

BakerBooks

a division of Baker Publishing Group
Grand Rapids, Michigan

Published by Baker Books
A division of Baker Publishing Group
P.O. Box 6287, Grand Rapids, MI 49516-6287
www.bakerbooks.com

Printed in the United States of America

Library of Congress Cataloging-in-Publication Data

Harney, Kevin.
    The u-turn church : new direction for health and growth / Kevin G. Harney and Bob Bouwer.
       p.   cm.
    Includes bibliographical references.
    ISBN 978-0-8010-1371-3 (pbk. : alk. paper) 1. Church growth. 2. Church renewal. I. Bouwer,
Bob. II. Title.
    BV652.25.H368   2011
    254'.5—dc22

                                           2011002510

Acknowledgments

A special thanks to the congregation of Corinth Reformed Church in Byron Center, Michigan. Your willingness to try new things, follow God in new ways, sacrifice for the sake of those not yet in God's family, and serve with passion was a key to the amazing U-Turn we experienced together.

—Kevin G. Harney

For the glory of God I thank Faith Church (RCA) for their obedience to God in reponse to the U-Turn process. From the humble beginnings in a gymnasium to campuses in Dyer, Cedar Lake, Valparaiso, Sheridan, and soon Hammond, you have been supportive and prayerful. You are truly an amazing church. I also thank my wife, Laurie, and my children, Courtney (and Joel), Caitlin, Grant, and Carley. You not only walked alongside me in this journey, but actively participated as servants yourselves. I would also like to thank my assistants, Mary Ann Van Amstel and Pam Gibson.

—Bob Bouwer

Contents

Introduction

Welcome to the Journey

Why Make a U-Turn?

Have you ever been driving down the road and suddenly realized you were heading in the wrong direction?

We all have.

What do you do when this happens?

The answer is simple. You look for the closest place to make a U-Turn. You get back on track.

Today, many people drive with a Global Positioning System. With the technology of a GPS, you would think none of us would ever get lost again, but this is not the case. It is still possible to end up heading in the wrong direction. If you have a voice-activated GPS, you know what happens in these frustrating moments. A pleasant voice says, *"Recalculating."* Then it gives you a new route.

A GPS helps you find the best route to get to your desired destination.

In the church, there are times when we could use a Spirit-led "recalculating" moment. We didn't mean to wander off, but something happened, and the church veered off course. Over time, it becomes clear that we need to move in a new direction. The old way of doing things is not working. The "tried and true" approaches are not bearing fruit. The call to "Go make disciples of all nations" (Matthew 28:19) is still in our hearts, but we don't see an influx of new believers coming into our local church. We want to see Christians grow into full maturity, but many seem to be on a spiritual *pause*.

In these moments we hear the voice of the Spirit saying, "Recalculate." God calls us to make a U-Turn and try a fresh new direction.

The gospel and truth of God's Word do not change, but the way we do ministry, our approach to worship, and how we reach our communities, need to be reexamined. This is the U-Turn moment many churches are facing today.

Maybe it is where you are right now.

You Are Not Alone!

If you look at your church and have a deep sense that something fresh and new needs to happen, you are not alone. If you hunger for a movement of the Holy Spirit that will lead to greater joy in your church, a season of harvest where souls are changed for eternity, and new passion in your own spiritual life, you are not alone. If your church has hit a plateau or is losing ground, you are in good company.

A majority of churches in the U.S. have stagnated or are declining. That is the sad truth.[1]

The focus of this book is to give hope as you enter a Spirit-directed U-Turn journey that will lead to a season of health, faithfulness, growth, and new vision. This is not a fantasy concocted by a couple of hyper-optimistic pastors who have no idea what they are talking about. The U-Turn journey is one the authors of this book have traveled and helped many other churches navigate.

We know there are congregations all over the U.S., and the world, that are longing to take new steps forward and move in fresh directions.

Sadly, they feel stuck.

Some are shackled by the chains of tradition and an unhealthy clinging to past ways of doing things. Others feel they lack the vision or leadership needed to move in a new direction. Still other churches worry that making a U-Turn will mean compromise of their commitment to God's Word, their denominational distinctions, or their cherished values. For some congregations, the very structure of their church government dictates against what it takes to make a U-Turn. These kinds of roadblocks can stand in the way of a church setting a new course for their future. In this book, we look at what stands in the way of local congregations thriving, and we offer very practical ways to move past these obstacles and into a new and hope-filled future.

The *U-Turn Church* will draw illustrations and lessons from two churches that have experienced healthy transformation over years of walking through a U-Turn strategy. Bob Bouwer will tell the story of Faith Church and Kevin Harney will share the journey of Corinth Church. Out of these two congregations, lessons will be gleaned that you can use in your process of making a U-Turn.

A Tale of Two Churches

Faith Church was a traditional, mainline church positioned in an urban area on the southern fringes of Chicago. It had passed its growth peak and was losing about twenty-five members a year. When they began their U-Turn journey, Faith Church had about two hundred seventy-five people in weekly worship.

Today, Faith Church is a vibrant and growing congregation with over four thousand worshipers gathering weekly in three weekend worship services on the main campus in Dyer, Indiana; a Sunday service on the Cedar Lake campus; a Sunday service on the Valparaiso campus; and in three on-site video-venue services called "The Well." Faith Church plans to begin four or five more multi-site locations in the next five years (with an intentional focus on growing the diversity of their congregation).[2] They have heard the call to train other congregations and leaders and have begun an organization called U-Turn Church Ministries.[3]

Corinth Church bought new land and built a new worship center, but was still struggling and stagnant when they approached their one-hundredth birthday. It was a small country church on the outskirts of Byron Center, which is on the edge of Grand Rapids, Michigan. Corinth Church was right in the middle of a farming community. In one hundred years of ministry they had grown from a handful of families to about two hundred fifty worshipers. They had used the same order of worship, morning and evening, for almost a century and were staunchly locked into a traditional mold.

Today, Corinth ministers to more than two thousand people in an average week with two contemporary services, a traditional service, an alternative service, and youth-based services. The campus of Corinth has three distinct worship venues, and each holds services of diverse styles.[4] Corinth has also birthed a daughter church, Wayfarer Community Church, that is impacting people in the Grand Rapids area.[5]

The U-Turn Church will teach through real-life examples drawn from Faith and Corinth Church. This book will offer a unique perspective as these two stories are told side-by-side. In many cases, similar practices and decisions led to equally effective U-Turn momentum. But in other cases, these two churches took different steps to keep moving forward. The juxtaposition of these two similar but distinct journeys will offer the reader varied lenses to look through. This will make it possible for many types of churches to see themselves in the narrative and receive vision, hope, and practical direction to begin their own U-Turn journey.

One thing you might notice as you read this book are some remarkable similarities in the stories of Faith Church and Corinth Church. How can that be? How could two different congregations, separated by over a hundred miles and a Great Lake, have almost identical experiences down to specific details? We attribute the similarity to three things: (1) We (the authors) are friends and would call each other from time to time and check in on ideas and how the journey was going; (2) we were influenced by the same leaders at that same period of time and attended many of the same conferences;[6] (3) the Holy Spirit was at work. The Spirit of God produced similar stories because He was doing a similar work in two churches that are part of a struggling and declining denomination.

Churches all over the world are facing decline, including in the United States. Most mainline denominations are struggling to figure out how to stem the tide of this erosion. Also, many independent and nondenominational churches are struggling with these same troubling realities.

Both churches studied in this book are part of the oldest existing denomination in the U.S.[7] The first worship and Communion service held by a small group that would one day become the Reformed Church in America took place in the small colonial town of New Amsterdam (now New York) in 1628. Though the Reformed Church has a rich history, there has been consistent decline for almost four decades. In the middle of this denomination-wide downward slide, both Faith Reformed Church and Corinth Reformed Church experienced and continue to enjoy what countless churches long for: new life, new hope, and lasting revitalization; in other words, a U-Turn.

Art and Science

Making a U-Turn demands the presence of the Holy Spirit, lots of prayer, patience, and wisdom. We are not telling anyone that if they do what Faith Church and Corinth Church did over the past two decades they will have the exact same results. The truth is, these two churches have their own distinct and unique stories.

We are not presenting a scientific model with a series of actions that you can follow and have the same results every time. We will, however, give many transferable principles that you can adapt to your unique environment. We believe, with prayer and wisdom, these ideas and guidelines will help you make an effective U-Turn.

The U-Turn journey is exactly that, a journey. Part of it is an art form. It is free flowing. When you are on your way you will learn things that we did not experience in our U-Turn. That is why we have set up the U-Turn Blog where we can continue to learn from each other.[8] We believe your distinct setting will demand an approach that looks something like what we experienced, but it will have unique twists and turns. Our intention in this book is to help you along the way. It is also to encourage you to discover how the general guidelines we have learned fit where God has placed you.

Our prayer is that you will experience a Spirit-directed recalculation that leads to a season of harvest beyond what your church has ever seen before. We believe God wants your congregation to enter a time of new depth in spiritual maturity, passion in worship, and fruitfulness in outreach.

To that end, we pray that this moment marks the beginning of something amazing for God's kingdom and joy-filled for your congregation.

In God's amazing grace and mercy,

Kevin Harney and Bob Bouwer

The Beginning of the U-Turn

You are not holding this book by accident.

God wants to take you on a journey that will shape your future, your life, your church, and the world in ways you can't yet imagine.

If you have ever gone hiking or backpacking in a remote desert or mountain area, you know there are vital things you need to take with you for the trek ahead: things like fresh water, nutritious food, a compass, appropriate clothing, a first-aid kit, a good trail map (or GPS), and other essentials.

As you embark on your U-Turn journey, there are a few things you will want to put on your checklist and be sure to pack:

- **Childlike Faith**—Know that God is with you each step of the way. Trust Him. Look for Him along the path. Listen for the Spirit's gentle whisper.
- **A Road Map**—God's Word in your heart and hand will be both a map for the journey and a lamp to light the way in the dark times.
- **An Innovative Spirit**—Get ready to experiment, try new things, and take a few risks. The more things you try, the greater your chance of

discovering something exciting and fresh. God might even invite you to travel a bit off the beaten path. Give it a try.

- **Company for the Journey**—Invite a friend or two to come along. As you read this book and begin the U-Turn adventure, make sure you do it in community.

Have a great trip!

1

Holy Zeal

by Kevin G. Harney

Great programs, a new strategy, and reading this book
are not enough to bring an enduring U-Turn experience to your church.
The essential piece in any real U-Turn is what we like to call holy zeal.

A true U-Turn is never birthed in the heart of a church leader or a desperate church board; rather, it comes from the loving heart of God. A U-Turn is not about saving our church, filling our worship center with more people, impressing our denominational leaders with our yearly report, or increasing our offering so we can pay the bills and keep our church afloat for another year.

A U-Turn is about the glory of God, the name of Jesus, the health of His bride (the church), and reaching a world that is in desperate need of a Savior. The only way a true U-Turn fire will be ignited and continue to burn is when the zeal of God's heart consumes us and we long for what He longs for.

What burns brightest in the heart of God?

What are His dreams?

What is the living God up to in the world these days?

God longs for His bride, the church, to be healthy and vibrant. He wants the local church to be a transforming presence in every community on the face of the earth. The God of heaven is waiting, ready to help your church be filled with His zeal so that His dreams become a reality right where He has placed your congregation.

That is the focus of our first chapter. If we get this part right, the rest will follow naturally.

If You Build It, They Will Come

Corinth Reformed Church had grown from about thirty people in worship to around two hundred fifty in the span of one hundred years. Okay, it was not a story of a meteoric rise in attendance, catching the attention of the editors of *Outreach* magazine as they updated their list of America's fastest-growing churches. The truth is, the church had grown by an average of two people a year for a full century and much of this growth came in the delivery room at a local hospital in Grand Rapids, Michigan.

Three families (by blood and marriage) made up almost half the congregation.

Byron Center is a small town, and the church building stood in the middle of a field in an unincorporated corner of the town, with only a handful of homes within a mile of the property. Almost anyone attending the church had to come either by horse and buggy or automobile, depending on whether they came at the beginning of the twentieth century or the end of it. It was not a city church, or even a suburban church. It was a country church.

In 1993, the congregation bought a good piece of land from a church member and built a new worship center that was almost three times larger than what they needed for an average Sunday. This got them out of the decaying one-hundred-seat traditional sanctuary just across the street and over the need to have two Sunday services. Being in a larger worship space made it possible to return to having just one service, which made everyone happy because they could see all their friends and feel like a close-knit family again. The only problem was, the congregation was rattling around in a worship space that fit them like an XXL jersey on an eighty-five-pound junior high football player.

They had acted on the *Field of Dreams* philosophy: "If you build it, they will come."

The only problem was, crowds did not flock to the new building.

A year before their centennial celebration, Corinth Reformed Church was in a beautiful new building with about the same number of people as they'd had in the little white-steeple church across the street. At the same time, they were actively searching for a new pastor to lead them into the future.

I received a phone call from the outgoing pastor. He was honest and blunt: "Can you come preach at Corinth? They want to check you out."

I said no rather quickly.

I was part of a growing ministry that had a rapidly developing evangelistic focus. We were in multiple services with multiple styles and were seeing many lives changed. I was not looking to make a move in my pastoral ministry.

The search team at Corinth Church was persistent. They came to me twice and asked me to consider being their pastor. Strike one and strike two! Each time, I explained that I was not open to a new call and ministry setting.

On their third try, they sent a team of three key church leaders to listen carefully to me and try to discover why I was not interested in being their pastor.

The answer was pretty simple. It had to do with "holy zeal."

I saw a good church, a nice new building, very sweet people, a strong commitment to the teaching of the Bible and rich tradition. But I did not see a burning passion for the heart of God and a dying world. My impression was that they wanted a new pastor to come and take care of them and help them continue on the same trajectory they had been on for the last century. They wanted to reach enough people to fill up their new worship space, but I did not see any real passion for souls.

I was sure of one thing: I was not the right pastor for the assignment.

When Clarence, Abe, and Dan came to my house on my day off to talk with me one more time, I was sure that strike three would make the point clear. They would know I was out of the picture, they would get the message loud and clear, and they would take their ball and go home!

I was wrong.

In that meeting in my basement office, I got a glimpse of a "holy vision" that burned deep in the heart of this small country congregation.

What is "holy zeal"?

Pure and simple, it is the heart of God beating in the heart of His people. It is a hunger for the glory of God to pour into a church and overflow into the community. It is a longing for more than a church "circling the wagons" so the world won't get in. It is a Spirit-prompted discontent with church being only about keeping the sheep in the pen and well fed. It is a burning desire to see people enter a relationship with the God who loves them and who entered human history to show them the way back home and into His arms. Holy zeal is a passionate commitment to count the cost, be willing to sacrifice, and follow Jesus into His ministry of making disciples of all nations.

Wrong Motives for Making a U-Turn

Any church can create a sense of momentum, and with enough energy, stem the tide of decline and create a movement of growth . . . for a brief time. But it will not endure and continue growing if the motives are wrong. As a matter of fact, there are times when God will intervene and stop the momentum of a church if the hearts of the people are not beating with His heart.

Self-preservation. One wrong motive for change is self-preservation. Many congregations want to make a U-Turn, reach out, and grow because they are desperate to survive. The idea that First Presbyterian Church might no longer be a presence on the corner of Maple and Lincoln is just too painful: "I was married in the sanctuary of this church." "Our children made a commitment to Jesus in the Sunday school rooms." "We have been here for too many years." "We simply can't tolerate the idea of our beloved church going under."

But merely wanting to survive cannot be called holy zeal. It will not lead to a sustained U-Turn.

Increased income. Another motive that drives a church to grow is to bring in more income. This might sound crass, but I have actually heard church leaders say things like, "We need more giving units in our church." They mean *people,* not units. But this kind of thinking motivates some church boards. They will try a few new tactics, introduce another program, or adopt a creative methodology to draw in a few more people to help pay the bills.

Larger attendance. Some churches consider making a U-Turn just to have an increase in attendance or numbers on the membership roll. The ego of a pastor or church leadership team can push some congregations to try whatever it takes to help them grow in numbers so they can feel good about themselves.

Though God surely wants churches to reach out and impact more and more lives with the grace and love of Jesus Christ, stroking the ego of leaders is not going to posture a church for a sustained U-Turn experience.

The Glory of God and the Name of Jesus

A U-Turn is first and foremost about lifting up one God: Father, Son, and Holy Spirit. It is about bringing the refreshing water of Jesus to a parched and thirsty world. The holy zeal that will move a church outward and upward is based on a desire to see people from every nation and tongue bow at the feet of Jesus and declare Him "Lord."

When Jesus is on the throne of a local church, holy zeal is in abundant supply. When we have forgotten our first love, this zeal is scarce.[1] As you think about your congregation or ministry, ask yourself, "Is there a passionate hunger to see Jesus lifted up and God glorified?"

If there is, you have some of the needed foundation for a U-Turn. But if your ministry has become focused on the people more than on the One who created the heavens and the earth, it is time to adjust your vision. If your church is content doing nice things for a group of nice people who all meet weekly to enjoy each other's niceness, you have lost your way and forgotten why the church exists.

The church is the bride of Jesus and He is the groom.[2] The bride must long for the groom and hunger for His name to be exalted and honored in every square inch of creation. Holy zeal comes when we actively seek to lift up the God who made us and loves us.

The Maturity of God's People

Holy zeal also grows when we seek to help God's people become truly mature in faith. A church that is focused on pampering believers and coddling Christ-followers will lack holy zeal. The apostle Paul sets the bar very high. He says that we are to help people become "mature, attaining to the whole measure of the fullness of Christ."[3]

Let that settle into your soul.

The vision of God is for us to continue being shaped and formed into the likeness of our Savior. This does not happen overnight. It does not come spontaneously as we wander aimlessly through life. Maturity comes as we walk with Jesus, feed on His Word, and live for Him in this world.

The more we are filled with His holy zeal, the more we will be like Jesus. As the Holy One of heaven is formed in us, His zeal becomes ours. His dreams fill our waking hours. His glory becomes our consuming passion. And we want the things that will most glorify Him.

A church that wants to make a serious and sustained U-Turn will call believers to new levels of holiness, faithfulness, and ministry. This happens in many ways, big and small, and we will explore these in the coming chapters of this book.

The Call to Scatter Seed

Jesus told a story about a farmer who went out to sow his seed. Instead of being careful and responsible, he just threw seed everywhere. This reckless farmer was counter-cultural. He was irresponsible. He was extravagant.

Seed was expensive. Farmers planted seeds with great caution and care. But the farmer in Jesus' parable scattered seed everywhere.[4] No doubt the farmer knew that every seed does not take to the soil as it should. The more seed planted, the greater chance of a good crop.

This is the call on the church. This parable is a picture of holy zeal. We are to bring the love and presence of Jesus to the world with extravagant abandon. It was the apostle Paul, one of the greatest evangelists in history, who reminded us that some of us plant seed, others water it, but only God can bring growth and change lives.[5]

Holy zeal is about finding new and creative ways to do what Christians have done for two millennia: scatter the seed of the gospel of Jesus Christ. A church that wants to make a U-Turn is not focused on "giving units," "self-preservation," or "ego-stroking." U-Turn churches know that God has opened the way to a restored relationship with Him through the sacrificial death of Jesus Christ on the cross. U-Turn churches have seen the glorious and resurrected Christ in their midst and they hunger for neighbors, friends, and even their enemies to meet this amazing Savior. U-Turn churches will do anything and everything to bring this good news to the ends of the earth and to the people next door.

Are you ready to start the journey of a God-honoring, Christ-exalting, Spirit-led U-Turn? How is your zeal factor? Is your church committed to lifting up Jesus and bringing glory to His name? Are you prepared to call new believers and longtime followers of Jesus to fresh places of commitment and maturity in their faith? Are you excited to see people meet Jesus for the first time and experience the joy, freedom, and wholeness that He alone offers?

Back in the Basement

I spent over two hours with Clarence, Abe, and Dan . . . and it was my day off! I tried to help them understand that the church exists not just to pamper those who are already part of God's family, but to reach out with the amazing grace of God to a lost and broken world.

They agreed.

I talked about how their way of doing church had not changed in ninety-nine years and that they might want to reexamine things and consider a little innovation.

They agreed.

I painted a picture of a growing community of believers that loved the lost and reached out to them. Their new building had a balcony that could seat over two hundred people, and there were not even seats in it. I asked them what they would do if the church grew to the point of needing to go to two services again. Rather than being daunted by the idea of seeing the church grow three times larger, they seemed to get excited at the thought.

Most of all, I talked about the holy zeal that burns in the heart of God for those who are still wandering like lost sheep.[6] I could see passion in the eyes of these three men. They wanted to be leaders in a church that honors God and grows believers but also reaches out with love and the message of Jesus.

After some honest and earnest conversation, they thanked me for my time.

I told them I was still not interested in coming to be their pastor, but that I had truly enjoyed our time together.

As the three men left my study, the last one out the door paused, looked me straight in the eye, and said, "You need to pray more! You are not hearing God right."

And with those words, he walked out.

U-Turn Exercises and Activities

U-Turn Exercise—The Highlighter Test

Sit down with a calendar of all your church activities for the coming two months and do what we call the highlighter test. Mark with one color everything that happens in your church that is primarily directed toward those who already know Jesus. Then with a second color, mark those things you do primarily for people who have still not entered into a life-giving relationship with the Savior.

After you have done this, do the same thing with your church budget. Mark with one color what you spend on things that are primarily for people who are already part of God's family. Then mark with a second color what you spend on ministry to people that are still wandering far from God.

Once you have your marked calendar and budget in front of you, reflect on where your priorities are as a church. Take the time necessary to talk with others about what these highlighted documents tell you about the focus and zeal of your church. Also pray for fresh vision and commitment to build a church that has a zeal that reaches beyond your church property lines.

U-Turn Reflection Questions

Gather with your leaders and key influencers in your church. Ask each one to read this chapter, and then reconvene to talk about the following questions:

- What is motivating us to make the desired U-Turn? Are we driven by healthy motives or by motives that won't sustain our journey?
- Was there a time when our church had a holy zeal for God and our community? If so, how have things changed?
- What are we doing now to bring the love and grace of God to our community? What steps could we take to be more engaged in communicating the life-saving message of Jesus?

U-Turn Prayers

Gather with church friends, leaders, or small-group members and pray in the following directions:

- Ask God to unleash a holy zeal in the lives of your staff and church leaders.
- Thank God for the faithfulness of leaders and laypeople in your church and the wonderful ways God has worked and moved in your midst in the past.
- Pray for a renewed commitment to lift up Jesus in all you do as a church and for a passion for the lost for the glory of God.
- Ask God to move every believer in your congregation to new places of maturity and to deeper commitment to personal spiritual growth.
- Pray that your church will become a mission outpost right where you are. Surrender your church to God's plan to reach out and make disciples in your community and everywhere else He may send you.

2

Urgency

by Bob Bouwer

U-Turn churches have a sense of urgency that moves them out of the status quo and beyond the "same old, same old" mindset.

We all know that not much happens until something becomes urgent. People don't usually worry about their health until their doctor tells them there is something significantly wrong with them. Then they are quick to seek a solution. If you have a serious financial problem, you will say to your financial advisor, "What are we going to do to fix this problem?" When something moves from the status quo to the urgent, things happen and things change.

That's part of the story of Faith Church. Our mindset moved from same old, same old to the urgent.

Some years ago, I learned this lesson on a very personal level. When our oldest daughter was quite young, she would come to us from time to time and say, "Mommy, Daddy, my heart is going fast." At first we kind of just ignored it, or we'd say, "Sweetie, you'll be okay. Don't worry about it. You were probably just running fast or maybe you're a little nervous." We really didn't take it too seriously. Then late one Saturday night, our daughter came into our room and said, "Mom and Dad, I don't feel good. My heart is really going fast." I nonchalantly took her hand and tried to count her pulse rate. Suddenly everything changed. Her heart was beating so fast I literally could not count the beats. We jumped into the car and took off for the hospital emergency room in the middle of the night. I remember calling the associate pastor at our church on the way and telling him he would have to preach for me the next day. When we arrived, the trauma nurse was calm and casually took notes as we told her what was happening with our daughter. But her casual demeanor changed when she took our daughter's wrist to measure her pulse. We could tell she was as shocked as we were. She could not count the heartbeats either, and what had been status quo for the nurse quickly became urgent. That urgency motivated the doctors to do medical tests and procedures that led to a correct diagnosis for our daughter. We thank the Lord that through modern medicine they were able to treat her condition and she leads a normal life of growth and health.

Fear-Induced Urgency

I had been at Faith Church a couple of years as the co-pastor when the senior pastor retired. I was now the thirty-year-old senior pastor, and scared out of my mind. While I loved the new responsibility I was facing, I was concerned as to how I was going to be able to pull it off. The truth is, I was confident on the outside but shaking on the inside.

Prior to our monthly board meeting, our executive committee met to set up the agenda. My first executive committee meeting was held at an Italian restaurant in Dolton, Illinois. The hostess led us to a booth in a back corner where we began to dialogue about the next week's agenda. Then the conversation shifted because someone brought up some of the complaints people had been having with small changes happening in the church. Then I noticed one of the board members was becoming very agitated. Without warning, he slammed his hand down on the table and said with barely concealed anger, "I just want you to know I have gone through our membership books and realized that over the last seven years we've lost an average of twenty-five members per year. If we don't do something soon we will be a dead church by the year 2012." He went on to say that most of those who left were young families or young singles.

I remember sitting in that booth and feeling a new sense of urgency. I gently proceeded with the agenda, quietly pondering what was ahead. That board member had no idea what his comments did to my insides. They rocked my world. I realized then that the church I was serving was worse off than I had first imagined. I guess I was living in a dream world. It had seemed okay, and all I needed to do was a little tweaking. But now I realized I had a choice to make. Either I needed to plan my escape route in the next couple of years and find another church, or respond to the calling and see if God could use me to move this church from a maintenance ministry into something greater.

Inside I felt a new sense of urgency. This moment became the genesis of Faith Church's U-Turn journey.

Again, nothing happens without a sense of urgency. For me, it became personal. When we examined our church, the urgency I felt was the catalyst that got me moving, praying harder, studying more, and leading smarter as we sought ways to turn our church around, because we were facing a very difficult future. If you are reading this, you have to wrestle with your own degree of urgency. Examine your church and ask, "What does our future look like?" "What do we want it to look like?" "Do we have a sense of urgency for the future of our church?" "What is my part in seeing change come about?"

Internal Urgency

Take your church's pulse. Start by looking at the number of people in your church. When I consult with churches, someone always says, "We don't care about numbers; we're not one of those number-counting churches." When I hear that, I feel bad because numbers are actually one of the ways for a church to discover their most urgent needs.

When a baby is born, hospital personnel do a series of tests to determine the health of the infant. Numbers talk, whether it's the child's weight, bilirubin count, or Apgar score. The parents are relieved when the numbers are good. You can imagine the urgency the parents feel when told the numbers are not good. Healthy numbers communicate good health.

Yet when a church is not growing, or is merely maintaining, or even declining, how can leaders say they're not into the numbers? The numbers could indicate a spiritual issue.

I think God is concerned about numbers because numbers represent souls. I remember hearing Rick Warren from Saddleback Church say, "If God wasn't into numbers, why would He name a book of the Bible after it?" He was joking of course, but he went on to say, "If God wasn't into numbers, why include three thousand as the number of people that came to Christ after Peter's sermon?"[1] Couldn't God just have said that many people came to know Christ after Peter's sermon? Of course not! God was thrilled to communicate that there was movement in His kingdom. There was growth, there were numbers, there were lives being changed as a result of Peter's preaching of the gospel.

The bottom line is that numbers do matter. Numbers can create a sense of urgency. Those numbers could represent growth, and that would give the body of Christ, the Church, the desire to deal with the issues resulting from the growing numbers.

I remember when Faith Church was experiencing tremendous growth and there was a need for more space, more seats, and more parking. Because we examined the numbers, we realized we needed to do something, and do it quickly. There should be the same sense of urgency in any church that looks at the numbers and sees a decline in membership, fewer professions of faith and baptisms, or a drop in giving.

When I consult with churches through U-Turn Church Ministries, we ask them to send us a spreadsheet of the numbers on their membership rolls, numbers of those attending on a given weekend, and numbers in children's or other ministries. Part of the U-Turn process is for them to see the decline in their numbers in any of these areas. Often churches live in a state of denial. They may say they have a church of fifteen hundred members on their rolls, but in reality they have only five hundred coming to worship. I urge churches to be honest about the numbers, because numbers speak the truth.

Even in my own ministry at Faith Church, my flesh would love to inflate those numbers. I'd love to feel better because of those numbers. I'm not a real big detail guy, and sometimes I underestimate or overestimate the numbers, but we have people who are watching our numbers all the time. We count the attendees in every worship service. We count the children in children's ministry, in youth groups, young adults, mini-churches (small groups), MOPS, women's Bible studies, and men's Bible studies. We look at all the ministries and ask, "How are we doing?"

Just recently we were looking at numbers and realized that one of the greatest growth areas in our church occurred in what we first considered an overflow section in our atrium, called "The Well." The Well contains seating for people to worship through a live video feed on a large screen. As we saw the numbers increasing, we realized the need to be more intentional about this space. We surveyed people on why they preferred to worship there. Our discoveries influenced our future decisions.

A wise church that is seeking to turn around does an honest assessment of their numbers, evaluates them, and asks, "What does this tell us?"

Eternal Urgency

While I believe it is important for a U-Turning church to examine their numbers, there is a greater purpose in doing so than simply seeing growth or decline. There's a spiritual urgency to assessing numbers because those numbers represent souls that are or could be transformed in Christ for eternity. It's not so much how we get there, but that we get there, period. Bill Hull says it well: "The traditional church is talking out of both sides of its mouth, giving a hearty 'amen' to the Great Commission and an entrenched 'no' to the changes required."[2]

I remember as a young Christian reading the book of Thessalonians and hearing Paul speaking about the second coming of Christ. He warned the church not to be idle. I was cut to the heart and could sense an urgency in my own soul. I knew that a part of the call of the gospel was to proclaim the good news of Jesus Christ because people's eternal destiny was at stake. In Matthew 24:45–46, Jesus teaches that the church must be ready for His return: *Who then is the faithful and wise servant, whom the master has put in charge of the servants in his household to give them their food at the proper time? It will be good for that servant, whose master finds him doing so when he returns."*

Part of the urgency in a church is to become aware of what is at stake in the gospel message for every person: to realize that Jesus Christ is coming again someday. Can you imagine if the Bible were to give the exact date when Christ would return? What if it were just two weeks away? Everyone who knows Christ would be desperate to say to loved ones, "You don't understand, He's coming back in two weeks!" There would be an all-out urgency that most of us do not sense on a regular basis. A U-Turn church understands the compelling need to share the message of heaven and hell and is fully convinced that someone who doesn't know Christ is facing an eternity *without Christ.* Those who know Christ know their responsibility to be the bearer of the gospel to those who are far from Christ. In my years at Faith Church, from time to time people would ask, "You know, Bob, aren't there enough people here now? Haven't we grown enough?" When I heard that, it would remind me that every person has an eternal soul and it would renew the call of Jesus Christ in me.

When there's a newfound urgency, things happen. I think of the story of Jonah. The Lord said to Jonah, "Go to Nineveh and preach, speak, and witness." He didn't think the people were worth it and chose to rebel. He ran from God and took a ship headed away from Nineveh. God sent a violent storm that forced Jonah to admit that he had rebelled. He was thrown overboard and swallowed by a giant fish. Inside the fish, he cried out to the Lord with a whole new sense of urgency. He finally realized what was at stake. He saw how important the people of Nineveh were to God. He realized he had a task to do for the Lord and he must do it.

That is what motivates me. It is what should motivate the church. There are people outside. People that matter to God so much that He gives His Church the sacred responsibility of sharing the gospel of Jesus Christ with them. I have neighbors who, from all outward appearances, are facing a Christ-less eternity. Their destination for all eternity is what motivates me. When I was forty-eight years old, I calculated that I was twenty-two years into ministry—about halfway through. The sense of urgency is still in me. I want my children and my grandchildren to be part of the bride of

Christ. I want them to be part of a church that delights in God, that seeks to witness to as many as possible for Jesus Christ.

New and Improved?

Maybe it's just me, maybe it's because I'm an American, maybe it's because I'm hyperactive, but I love anything that's new. I love new running shoes, new gadgets like cell phones and iPods and i-Whatever-It-May-Be. The U-Turn process entails newness and the need for constantly creating new things. New is exciting. New is challenging. New is invigorating. New is stimulating. And for us, the Church, part of the key is to figure out the new.

At a conference, I once heard Andy Stanley, pastor of a mega-church outside of Atlanta, give an interesting illustration. On a table he had displayed ten or fifteen bottles of Tide laundry detergent. He made it comical and said that as a kid he remembers that there was just one version of Tide. You would go to the store and you would buy Tide. Period. Tide was good. Tide did the job. Tide was the only option. Today if you go into a store and go to the laundry detergent section, you will see a variety of Tides. There's regular Tide, Tide with bleach, Tide with softener, Tide that smells like mountain air, Tide that smells like beautiful lavender, a new sports Tide, etc. He made his point. He said, what's interesting is that the makers of Tide are constantly creating something new. They recognize that people are intrigued by what's new. They are zealous to increase their market share. Newness brings fresh excitement to the marketplace. Newness is a tool used to meet what people consider an urgent need.

When we began our U-Turn process, one of the things we did was offer a new experience in worship. I went door to door through our neighborhood with about a hundred people from our church, placing flyers on doorknobs. We went into several area towns and the local mall and handed out flyers, inviting people to a new experience in worship. I was amazed at how many people came. When some of them were asked why they came, they said they were looking for something new.

Most people are intrigued by something new and want to try it. But not everyone is excited by new. Some people actually run from it. Some avoid it at all costs. When you're wrestling with people who don't want to change, you might help them become aware that in every area of life they are continually trying new things. We used to roll down our car windows by hand, but then came automated windows. We used to have fans to keep us cool, and then air-conditioning was invented. We change the style of our clothes when the new styles come in. The process of the U-Turn journey is to embrace the new. People outside the church will say the old church didn't work for them but they would consider something new. New is good.

A word of warning: *New* does not necessarily mean "improved." Just because it's new doesn't mean it is God's plan for you or even that it is right. Make sure the new is biblically sound. Make sure you have prayed through it before you adopt it.

The Urgency to Seek Outside Resources

The church that understands urgency is a church that is always seeking to learn from others how to expand the kingdom of God. The leaders of these churches are reading books like this one, learning how to grow and how to reach those that are far from God. These leaders attend interactive conferences, visit other churches to see how they do things, always wrestling with the best way to reach people with the message of Jesus Christ.

One of the things we did in the process of our U-Turn story was to set aside a portion of our budget each year for conferences. We believe it is important for people to attend conferences and seminars that teach about expanding God's kingdom. God has placed on all of us a huge responsibility to be witnesses for Him.

Recently four leaders from our church went to the Exponential Conference in Orlando, Florida. The central theme was church planting and member multiplication, and these guys came back on fire. They called me while they were gone and said, "Bob, we're dangerous. We have a bunch of new ideas." They came back with a new focus on the kingdom of God. They had just spent three days with more than three thousand church leaders from around the world who were excited and well-versed in terms of the call of the gospel. When leaders begin to see the urgency of the gospel in a new way, they will experience a shift in the focus of their church.

The Urgency of Communication

After you've looked at and wrestled with personal priorities, the priorities of your church, and our collective eternal priority, the next priority is to look at communicating the urgency of getting the message out. This communication begins in the pulpit. We began by doing a series of messages about reaching beyond our immediate group of believers. How do we reach lost people around us? What is the call in the Scriptures? We looked at the book of Acts, the story of Jonah, the call of Christ to go into all the world, and sought to educate our people through the preaching of the Word of God about what our focus should be.

Then we moved to fervent prayer. We invited the church into concentrated prayer for the lost. We had days of fasting and prayer for upcoming events in the church, praying that people from outside the kingdom of Christ would come. We gathered and prayed in small groups, asking people to wrestle with the urgent need before us.

We communicated through e-mails to the congregation, asking them to pause and pray for our upcoming series, giving them specific things to pray for.

We printed cards and handed them out to the congregation, asking them to use the cards to invite people to the next series. Verbally inviting a neighbor, co-worker, or friend to church is not comfortable for everyone, but most people are okay with handing out an invitation. The pressure of the invite is taken off of them and onto the church who printed the invitation. We found this to be an extremely helpful outreach tool.

We communicated the upcoming message series through our monthly newsletter, "In the Loop." Communication helps "rally the troops" and gets people talking about the messages in their daily lives, in small groups, in the ministries of the church, and in the leadership of the church. Our children's ministry, junior/senior high, and college-age ministries would often discuss the same topic at the same time. This resulted in the unity of our entire congregation, allowing us to move ahead with diligence by focusing together on the urgent things of God.

From Fear-Induced Urgency to Fruitful Urgency

From that meeting in the corner of a restaurant, God was doing a new thing in me and consequently in the ministry at Faith Church. Within the first year in our new building, 375 people joined Faith Church. That was new to us. New life, new problems, new staff, new, new, new! The next year we experienced the same rate of growth. Within five years, 2,000 new souls had become members of Faith Church.

We began to realize our facility had reached capacity, and we said, "Now what?" We hired a consultant who, after much study, came to our leadership and said, "You are behind the proverbial eight ball. You need more seats soon. You will begin to plateau quickly if you don't do something."

Once again, we were faced with an urgent need. The consultant presented us with a new concept. He told us, "You should multi-site." Our response: "What's that?" He explained that you take 100 to 150 of your people, willing to move to another site, such as a high school auditorium or gymnasium, offer live music, children's ministry, a campus pastor, and put the message on a video screen. Five years ago, that was new! New to me and new to our leaders, but our sense of urgency motivated us to continue. The consultant introduced us to Community Christian Church in Naperville, Illinois, and their New Thing Network—a group of churches who were also growing into the multi-site movement. We launched our first multi-site in a high school in Cedar Lake, Indiana, eleven miles southeast of our Dyer campus. Looking back, we got so much more than just extra seats. A whole new church was born. New people were drawn in from the community. Volunteers stepped forward to set up and take down the gym for worship, to sing, to play instruments, to work in the children's ministry, to operate the technology equipment, serve coffee, greet, usher, staff the welcome center, the bookstore, and more.

In 2009, we were approached by a church in Valparaiso (about forty-five minutes east of us) that was disbanding and asking if we would be interested in purchasing their church building and property. After some discussion, much prayer, and securing pledges to fund the purchase, we officially opened Faith Valparaiso on Easter Sunday 2009. It was a luxury to open the doors each week without having to set up chairs and truckloads of other equipment as we did while meeting in the school gym.

It still blows me away how our most recent campus, in Sheridan, Illinois, was started. It began with two couples who were passionate about sharing the love of Christ. One of the couples lived an hour and a half away from Faith Church's Dyer campus. They were strong believers stuck in a declining church. They wanted to worship God. They wanted their three young girls to grow up in a church that was alive. They came to us with a proposal to start a church in the loft of their barn, using a DVD of our Saturday night service. They have grown in less than a year to more than sixty worshipers every week. They outgrew the loft, and are now worshiping in a larger building on their farm. They have seen radical conversions. They have seen lukewarm Christians become on fire for Jesus. As I am writing this, I am preparing to facilitate a new members' class for more than twenty adults from their church. We wanted them to know that we supported them, so we asked them what they needed, and they said they could use a better screen to show the DVDs. They were using four shower curtains taped together! We gladly gave them a screen that very day. I never would have imagined that one of our campuses would be completely functional with a DVD, from music to message. And many people are alive in Christ Jesus today because we embraced these new ways of connecting people to Him.

Embracing the new does something. It's a catalyst. It moves us. It makes us depend on God. It makes us pray more. It makes us think biblically, theologically, purposefully. The new is good! The reward of new is inspiring. It makes you thirsty for more.

Today we have five campuses, and our denomination has asked us to start eleven new campuses by 2020. A new sense of urgency reigns at Faith Church!

God has been introducing new things since the foundations of the earth. When I see new technology, or even new songs for worship, I see God behind it, making all things new.

The church will be faced with new things until the final new thing happens. That ultimate new thing is when Christ returns. God is saving His big finale for that day. Revelation 21:1, 5 says, "*Then I saw a new heaven and a new earth. . . . He who was seated on the throne said, 'I am making everything new!' Then he said, 'Write this down, for these words are trustworthy and true.'*" It will be totally new, unlike anything we have known here.

Until that day, the church celebrates what God is doing. He is using His Church to bring new life and ultimate glory to His name.

Conclusion

When a church feels a sense of urgency, they will change. They will seek to learn from others how to make a difference. Often churches say they want to grow, but are reluctant to embrace the changes necessary to make it happen. To them, it is not urgent. I read recently that America is the fourth most un-churched nation in the world. If that doesn't seem urgent, I don't know what does. If we don't change, if we don't sense the need to change, do you know what the American church will look like? Western Europe. The American church is just years behind what European churches are like—empty.

That sense of urgency moves me to change, to pray, to do whatever I can to see God's bride renewed. *"The Spirit and the bride say, 'Come!'"* [3] And Jesus' response to His bride is "*Yes, I am coming soon.*"[4]

U-Turn Exercises and Activities

Prayer for Urgency

Father, give me a heart for what your heart is urgent for. Jesus, give me the same urgency for your church that brought you to the cross. Holy Spirit, fill me with the flame of urgency and the strength to change. Help me to embrace the new so that those who are far from you see the light of Christ in a healthy church. O Lord, match my urgency to yours, through Christ our Lord. Amen.

U-Turn Reflection Questions

After reading this chapter, gather with some leaders from your church and discuss the following questions:

1. When in your life as a pastor/leader did you sense some degree of urgency?
2. What are you presently urgent about?
   personally
   spiritually
   in your church
3. What do you sense your congregation is currently urgent about?
4. What do you think the church should be urgent about?
5. How do you best communicate the need for urgency?
6. How often do you think about the urgency of the second coming of Christ?
7. When was the last time your church had a sermon, conversation, and strategic plan for reaching people outside of the kingdom of God?

3

Crystal-Clear Vision

by Kevin G. Harney

Zeal and urgency are a gift . . .
only when we are heading in the right direction!

A church can have zeal and a deep sense of urgency, but can still be heading rapidly and passionately in the wrong direction. If we are going to make a healthy and sustained U-Turn, we must know the right destination. The clarity for this new direction comes when we have a crystal-clear vision of where God wants us to go.

Interviewing the Congregation

Corinth Church had come to me three times and asked if I would consider being their new pastor. I had told them no three times. After the meeting in my basement that ended with the firm exhortation to "pray more" because I was "not hearing God right," I did pray.

Actually, I first went to my wife and told her I was a little surprised by one of the men who told me he thought I was not really listening to

God. My wife's response was short and direct, "Well, maybe you do need to pray more."

So I prayed.

In time, I agreed to preach at Corinth Church so that I could get to know the congregation a little better. They were confident they wanted me to be their pastor, but I was not sure this was where God wanted me. I decided to make the most of the time and asked if I could interview their congregation after I preached. They seemed a bit surprised by the request, but said yes.

I requested that the entire congregation from high school students through the adults gather in the worship center after the morning service. For about an hour and a half I shared what I believed was a biblical vision for the church. My communication style is pretty straightforward so I really laid out what I believe the church exists to do. During this time, I cast a vision for what I believed God wants for every Christian congregation. I was clear that if I came to be their pastor, there were very specific things that we would commit to do and pursue together.

Some elements of the vision I shared were basic Bible 101. I emphasized that the church must always be built on the Word of God . . . with no compromise. Everyone seemed to like this emphasis.

I also spoke about the call to reach the community with the message of God's love and the good news of Jesus' life, death, and glorious resurrection. They were still with me.

I emphasized the importance of worship led by the Spirit of God. No one resisted.

Then I said that every member of the church would have to make a choice to sacrifice for the sake of the kingdom and be ready for dramatic change if we were to truly fulfill the Great Commission and reach our community with the gospel. This was met with some cautious stares and furrowed brows.

I clarified and pushed a little harder. I held up my Bible and said, "If Corinth Reformed Church really wants to be God's people in this community, you must hold this book as your final and absolute authority." Then I said these fateful words: *"Everything else is up for grabs!"* I pointed to the pulpit and said, "This is just furniture, there is nothing sacred about it." I placed my hand on the Communion table and said, "We do not worship this piece of wood. We worship the One whose body was broken and whose blood was shed for our forgiveness." I declared, "This building is simply bricks and mortar; it is a place to gather as God's people, but it is not the church . . . you are!" Most of the people seemed to get what I was saying, but there was a feeling of caution in the air.

At the time, I didn't know that the pulpit (which was quite large and foreboding) was never moved from its central and prominent position. In the same way, the Communion table and baptismal font had assigned places in the front of the church. I later heard a story about a man who had inadvertently placed something on the Communion table and had received a scathing rebuke from one of the church elders. With almost a hundred years of tradition and very set ways of doing things, I was lining up some sacred cows for slaughter. And I wasn't even their pastor . . . yet.

I told those gathered that if they truly wanted to reach the lost in their community, it would mean more change and challenge than any of them had ever dreamed of. It would mean "giving up" their church and letting people who came for the first time know that they are just as welcome as someone who had been part of the church for three or four generations.

At one point during the interview, I looked at my wife and realized that I was coming on pretty strong. My wife, Sherry, was born and raised in West Michigan, and she is a pretty good barometer of how church people in that part of the country think and feel. The mirror of her face was reflecting back a message loud and clear!

Her eyes were not telling me to stop, or even to back off. But I could see that she thought I was pushing pretty hard. I wanted these people to see a vision of a church so in love with God and passionate for the lost that they would do anything (within the bounds of Scripture) to reach the broken, hurting, and wandering sheep in their community. The truth is, I did not think God was going to call me to serve as their pastor. But I did want to shake them up a bit and cast a vision for what could be, if they were willing to count the cost, take up their cross, and follow Jesus into His mission.

I also asked the congregation a number of questions about their willingness to share their church, try new things, and question traditions that no longer served God, the church, or the world.

At the end of this extended interview, I invited everyone there to send me a letter and let me know if they believed I was called to be their pastor. I even said, "You do not need to sign the letter. I will still read it." I explained that normally I never read an unsigned letter, but in this case, I wanted them to be free to speak their mind anonymously.

What shocked and amazed me was that we received letters every day for the next week, and all of them had the same tone and feel. People had caught the vision and believed it was from God. There were concerns and sensitivities expressed, but the heartbeat of *every single letter* was, "We want to do God's will in our community and we will do whatever it takes to accomplish His purposes."

I am sure you have figured out by now that God did, indeed, call me to pastor this small country church in the middle of unincorporated Gaines Township, just outside of Byron Center, Michigan. For more than thirteen years I served Corinth Reformed Church, and it was a season of joy, fruitfulness, and adventure. During this time, the vision God had for us grew clearer and clearer with each passing year.

Putting It Into Words

Many churches express their vision and mission in a sentence or a series of simple statements. Some use alliteration (words that begin with the same letter) to make it memorable. Others try to keep the vision as short as possible.

As I began my ministry at Corinth Church, we gathered leaders and committed church members to work on clarifying, with words everyone could understand, why we existed. We were seeking to answer the question, "What is our vision?"

We looked at the statements of many other congregations and learned from them. Finally, we put our vision in words that worked for our people. This statement was designed to guide people who were already followers of Jesus, so we used language that connected with them. When it was all said and done, we ended up with five simple declarations. This is still the vision that guides all that Corinth Reformed Church does:

We exist to . . .
Exalt *God through Worshiping in Spirit and Truth*
Edify *Believers through Teaching and Admonition*
Enfold *Believers in a Loving Church Family*
Equip *God's People for Ministry*
Evangelize *the Unsaved with the Good News of Jesus*

Because this statement is designed to guide believers, we felt free to use words like *Admonition* and *Evangelize*. Your church might word things differently, but every congregation that wants to make a world-impacting U-Turn needs to put their vision into words that their church members understand. This way, if anyone asks, "What is your church all about?" you can show them your vision statement and there will be no question about what it means. When a new person joins the church, you can walk them through your vision statement, and they will have no question about where the church is headed.

For Corinth Church, this vision statement became the guideline for all action. Before any ministry at the church set a new direction, started a new program, or invested time and funds into something, they had to make sure they were in sync with the church vision. If the new idea did not support the vision, the answer was no.

Over time, the church came up with a short line that described the heart of the church. It was another way to keep the focus of the church on the bull's-eye of God's design. It is simply:

We exist to glorify God by introducing people to Jesus Christ and developing believers into fully devoted followers of Jesus.

This shorter statement tightens up the vision and helps people remember exactly why the church exists. The church is about lifting up God, growing believers, and reaching the lost.

The truth is, many churches have these kinds of statements on the records. Some time in their history, the church gathered a group of people to write a statement, or the pastor crafted some kind of vision declaration. But sadly, it is not guiding the practice and direction of the church.

If a church is going to function with crystal-clear vision, it needs to be in writing. But it also needs to be on the front burner of the church ministry at all times. Everyone must know it. Leaders must follow it. And this vision needs to guide the direction of all the church ministries.

Clarifying and Spreading the Vision

Over the coming decade at Corinth Church, we identified a number of principles for getting God's vision deep into the fabric of the local church. Here are some of the lessons we learned that I believe can be transferred to any church or Christian organization as they seek to move forward with a crystal-clear vision.

1. Remain biblical to the core.

If you look at the five elements of Corinth's vision, you will see that each one is based solidly on the teachings of the Bible. As you develop a vision statement for your church, support everything with Scripture. If it is not a central theme in the Bible, don't include it. If it is, make sure the whole church knows both the vision and the biblical bedrock it is built on. If it is only the vision of a leader or a church board, it will always waver and fail. It must be God's vision, not ours. We don't set the direction and vision and instruct the Creator of heaven and earth to make it so! We seek the vision God has for us and we fulfill His purposes.

When we follow the calling of God and have a vision that reflects His heart, it does not change every six months with all the new trends and innovations that come on the church radar. To be clear, the church must always innovate and try new things, but what we are doing is seeking new ways to spread the never-changing message of faith and hope that is found in Jesus alone.

The church I serve today is Shoreline Community Church (*www.shore-linechurch.org*). Our vision statement is simple, biblical, and crystal clear: *To help as many people as possible become totally committed to Jesus Christ.* If something does not fit into that vision, we do our best to set it aside and keep our main thing God's main thing.

If your church does not have a vision statement, develop one, and make sure it is biblical. Use the examples in this chapter, look on the Web sites of other churches, and call leaders you respect and draw from their wisdom. Study the Bible and make sure you are in concert with the teachings of God's Word. Don't just adopt the wording of another church. Make sure you shape a vision statement that fits your congregation.

If your church has a vision statement, test it against the teaching of the Bible. If it is biblical, use it, teach it, and let it guide your church. If it is not, change it!

A friend of mine was hired to serve a church in Southern California. They wanted to reach out, they wanted to grow, and they were willing to try some new things.

Well, that's what they said before they hired him.

When he got there, he discovered a different reality. Things were set in stone a bit more snugly than he was led to believe.

As he prepared to lead a U-Turn movement and help the church move outward, he bumped head-to-head with their vision statement. He knew it needed to be changed. It was too limited. It did not have the open-armed world focus that a good vision statement needs. And, it was not biblical.

He recommended they consider changing their vision statement. You would think he had suggested that the church sacrifice kittens on the Communion table during worship services. There was a huge revolt and resistance.

To put things in context, you should know their vision statement. It was quite clear:

> *First Reformed Church exists to minister to the*
> *Dutch Reformed Christians in our community.*

Do you get a sense of why my friend felt there was a need to tweak the vision statement a bit? It was exclusive on multiple levels and had no focus on those who were still outside of faith and the church. In essence, it was not big enough.

When they told him they were not open to tinkering with the vision statement, he told them he would be finding a new church to serve. This got their attention. Just as Bob wrote about in the last chapter, things suddenly became urgent and they were willing to look at things in a new way! My pastor friend explained that crystal-clear vision was so important that it was a deal breaker for him.

By God's grace, they reconsidered. My friend led a retreat where they expanded the breadth of their vision to reach and minister to people who were not Dutch, Reformed, Christian, or in the community. This marked the beginning of a whole new season of fruitful ministry for their congregation.

2. Get and keep your leaders and key influencers on the same page.

Both staff and volunteer leaders need to embrace the biblical vision God has given your church. It should be committed to memory by board members, key volunteers, and any and all staff members. If it is too long to memorize, consider revising it and tightening it up.

Every time a new idea pops up, board members should ask, "Does this support the vision God has given our church?" Staff members should use the vision of the church as a measuring rod for all they do. If something seems fun, cool, new, or worth a try, but it does not reinforce the vision of the church, don't do it.

This means the church pastor (or pastors) needs to come back to the church vision over and over and over. Then they need to review it again.

If a leader does not support the vision, he should not be leading in that church. It is just that simple. A church that keeps staff, board members, or key volunteers in places of influence when they do not support the vision is asking for trouble. We need to do all we can to educate and draw people into the vision, but if a leader is consistently fighting the clear vision God has given your church, then that leader needs to find a different place to serve.

3. Remind and review . . . often.

Vision leaks!

It really does. Over time, people forget why the church exists. This is why we need to remind people of the vision on a regular basis. Because it is biblical and core to our faith, believers will never get tired of hearing it.

At Corinth Church, we did a five-week preaching series on the church vision every single year I was there. The church still does this. Of course, you need to be creative and look at new facets and nuances, but each and every year the whole congregation should get a refresher course on the church vision. Because it is being preached, the biblical underpinnings can be communicated with clarity.

Along with a yearly congregational learning time, it is important to teach and remind people of all ages about God's vision for the church, including the children and youth. At Corinth, the vision statement was shaped to fit every ministry and every age group.

Too many congregations operate with the idea that the youth should "do their own thing" and the children "are too young to really get it." This does not lead to a strong and unified church. Once you have a clear vision statement, teach and review it often with everyone in the church.

4. Guard the front door.

One way you can keep the vision strong in your church is by guarding the front door. This is about making sure that all the new people who connect with the church understand the vision and buy into it.

When I was in seminary, one of my professors asked this interesting question: "When is the best time to lose an unhappy church member?" He went on to answer his own question: "Before they join!"

If someone is considering becoming a member of your church or connecting on a deeper level, be sure they know exactly what your church is about. Let them know about the crystal-clear vision you have and how you are seeking to follow this vision. Then if they jump in, they know what your church is all about.

At Corinth Reformed Church, this was done through a dynamic process of a three-generation membership class. We actually developed a class for children, another one for teens, and a third one for adults. All three generations were covered. We blocked off a good chunk of a Saturday each quarter to hold a class for those who wanted more information about the church and who were considering membership. This was required for all those who wanted to pursue formal membership and encouraged for all those who were becoming regular attendees. Even people who had been part of another Bible-believing church for years were required to come if they wanted to become members. The truth is, some of the most resistant people were those who had a long history of church attendance. They felt they had all the answers to church life. But we wanted them to know God's vision for Corinth Church.

We made the class fun and interesting. We shared a meal together. And we had the classes for children, youth, and adults simultaneously. Each of the classes was built around the framework of the five elements of the vision statement. This way everyone covered the same content, but in an age-appropriate manner.

By the end of the class, everyone knew the vision of the church. They knew what we were about. If they decided to join or come on a regular basis, there was no question about where we were going as a church.

I even did a short talk for the adult class called "Ten Reasons You Might Not Want to Join This Church." I played off the Jeff Foxworthy comedy bit "You just might be a redneck if . . ." I would say, "You just might not want to join this church if . . ." This was my chance to make it clear that because we had a clear vision, there would be some things we would not be doing.

In this talk I would let people know that worship was about glorifying God, not giving them what they wanted every time we gathered. I would say, "If you want worship services that always give you the style of music you want and a message that fits you perfectly, you just might not want to join this church." I talked about the vision that every believer would be equipped and deployed into a place of ministry where they were gifted. I would say, "If you are looking for a church that will meet your every need and not ask for anything back, you just might not want to join this church." You get the point.

Any church that has a clear vision and wants it to guide their ministry will find a way to educate and inspire those who are new to the church. If you guard the front door, you will be sure the people who connect with the church get the vision, believe in it, and are ready to support it.

5. Bless the past as you move into the future.

As you move forward into God's vision for the future, be sure to bless and celebrate the past. God has worked in great ways in your church for years, decades, or maybe even centuries. Don't shame the past. Thank God for it, celebrate it, and remember it. But move forward where God is leading.

When I was in seminary, a very wise pastor named Harold Korver invested in a number of the students. When he would talk about our future leading in the local church, he had a memorable and recurring line he would speak: "If you damn their past, they will damn your future. If you bless their past, they will bless your future." This reminder woke me up to the fact that we can celebrate all the good in the past, and we should, as we move forward.

If your church has not worked with a clear vision statement, don't curse the past. God was there. He was at work. Lives have been blessed and impacted by God all through the history of your church. Look back and be thankful. Celebrate what He has done. But don't live in the past. Move forward.

6. Do less to accomplish more.

When you know what your vision is as a church, you know what you should do. When Corinth Church declared, "We exist to evangelize the unsaved with the good news of Jesus," it moved us to do creative outreach. When the church agreed that their vision would include, "Enfolding believers into a loving church family," it clarified that we would commit to developing a culture of fellowship and community where believers would feel connected and loved. Each part of the vision said, "This is who we will be!"

At the same time, a vision statement also clarifies what we will not do and who we will not be. Because Corinth Church embraced the biblical vision to "Equip God's people for ministry," we were led to stop doing some things for people that they should be doing for themselves. One example was developing a lay care ministry where church members were trained to care for each other. This meant the church pastor would not be doing all of the hospital calling and shut-in ministry. It meant change. And some people did not like it! But our vision guided us in what we would do and not do.

Sometimes in the church we have to let things die. There are ministries that have been around for a long time. They were fruitful five, ten, or fifty years ago. Now they are on life support. If a ministry is no longer fulfilling the vision of the church, we should give it the dignity of a burial and let it go.

When a church is guided by a crystal-clear vision, we find ourselves doing less instead of more. Because we run every new idea through the grid of the church vision statement, we say no to some things. In some seasons, we say no to a lot of things. This does not mean they are not important. It does not mean they were not valuable in the past. It simply means they do not fit what God is doing in our midst right now.

Wise churches learn to do less busy stuff so they can do more of what matters most.

7. Be specific, concise, and measurable.

Once you have a vision statement, you can use it to set specific and measurable goals. When Corinth Church committed to passionately pursue God's vision to "Evangelize the unsaved," we began to ask a whole new set of questions. For instance, as the church grew numerically, we wanted to know if we were just seeing people from other congregations jump into what was happening at our church or if there was true conversion growth. So we measured it.

What we discovered was that over a third of the new people who were coming to the church were brand-new believers. This was exciting. In one year, over thirty people came as they confessed faith in Jesus Christ for the first time. We also learned that about a third of the new people coming were rededicating their life to Jesus. They had a Christian heritage or background, but had wandered away. As they connected at the church and caught God's vision, their faith was reignited and they were growing again. The third group was people who lived in the area or had moved into the area and were looking for a new church home. We were glad to welcome them in, but were sure to let them know the vision of the church so we could pursue it together.

The point of measuring the results of the vision is not so we can pat ourselves on the back and say, "Aren't we wonderful!" Rather, it is so we can know we are fulfilling the clear calling of God on our church.

At Corinth, there is a vision to "Equip God's people for ministry." This is measurable. We can ask how many adults in the church are serving God (in the church or outside of the church) in a way that uses their God-given gifts, impacts others, and brings glory to God. When I left the church, we had determined that over 65 percent of the adults were doing some kind of ministry. That led us to celebrate (because many churches have around 10 percent). It also led us to strategize over how we could equip and mobilize the other 35 percent.

Being specific and measurable in how we live out the vision helps a local church celebrate the wonderful work God is doing. It also clarifies where we need to put more energy and strive harder to fulfill the great calling God has placed on the local church.

Holy zeal ignites a passion in our hearts. Urgency gets us moving forward. Crystal-clear vision shows us where we are going. Too many congregations get fired up by every new ministry fad, but they don't have a sense of following God's enduring purpose for their ministry.

It is time for local churches to dig into God's Word, get on their knees in prayer, and clarify God's vision. Then we can pursue this with all the strength God places in us.

When I interviewed the congregation of Corinth Church almost two decades ago, they had zeal and urgency. What they needed was to clarify the vision and go after it. Today, that small country church ministers to over two thousand people in a normal week. They have planted a daughter church. They have multiple services with varied styles, but all of these worship gatherings have one purpose: "To exalt God through worshiping in spirit and truth." Their commitment to evangelism and missions has led them to give more money toward outreach each year than the entire budget was when I became the pastor.

The vision is becoming a reality. God is being lifted up. Believers are growing, serving, caring, and sharing. And lost people are coming home to Jesus. This is a U-Turn that brings joy to the heart of God and to His people.

U-Turn Exercises and Activities

U-Turn Exercise—Put It in Writing

Gather a group of leaders and key influencers and begin a process of writing a vision statement. Look at examples of churches you respect. Make sure your statement is biblical to the core. Use language that will speak to your church and culture.

Once you have a vision statement shaped, pray over it. Test it against Scripture, and refine it.

When you believe you have the vision God wants for your church, begin to share it. Use the ideas in this chapter to guide you.

U-Turn Exercise—Guard the Front Door

Take time to evaluate your membership process. Or, if your church does not have formal membership, evaluate how you connect and educate new attendees. In particular, look to see if your church vision is communicated with crystal clarity to these new people. Take the steps needed to make sure all the new people coming to your church have a clear picture of the church vision and know how they can enter in and support it.

U-Turn Reflection Questions

Gather some leaders and key influencers from your church (ask each one to read this chapter ahead of time), and talk about the following questions:

- If someone stood up in your church and said, "Except for what we find in the Word of God, everything else is up for grabs," what are some of the things people might rush to hold on to?
- Are our church leaders on board with the vision and supporting it with

their prayers, time, energy, and finances? What can we do to bring our leaders into closer alignment with the church vision?

- What are some of the great things God has done in and through your church in the past?
- What are some of the things your church might need to stop doing if you are going to give your full attention to God's vision for your future?

U-Turn Prayers

Gather with church friends, leaders, or small-group members and pray in the following directions:

- Ask God to make His vision for your church crystal clear, and for your congregation to pursue it with unyielding passion.
- Pray for the vision God has for your church to go deep into the lives of those who are members or regular attendees of your church. Pray for the adults, the youth, and the children. Every age group is a vital part of the church.
- Thank God for the past work He has done in your church. Remember faithful leaders from the past and give God praise for them. Celebrate the fruit God has grown in lives, homes, and your community through the years.
- Pray for the next season of your church's ministry to bring measurable and abundant fruit for the glory of Jesus!

4

The Power of Prayer

by Bob Bouwer

"My house will be a house of prayer." Matthew 21:13

Prayer is one of the most powerful tools God uses to change a church. Prayer is when the supernatural (God) collides with the natural (us). Prayer is where God intersects with humans; and when He does, there is powerful change. In the book of Acts, prayer is the movement that shook the house. Too often churches do not pray like that or believe like that, yet they expect God to move like that. God comes where He is invited. Prayer is that invitation.

All churches pray, but could they be called a house of prayer? Do their prayers merely begin and conclude a meeting? Are the real prayers only voiced at the midweek prayer meeting? Both the churches we have been writing about discovered a different kind of prayer. It's hard to describe because its basis is not a formula; it does not come out of a book, although there is nothing particularly wrong with that kind of prayer. It's as if we finally joined with God and He joined with us. There is urgency in it; faith, humility, dependency. This is not to say these churches have become perfect pray-ers, but we definitely pray differently than we did before our U-Turn.

Desperate Prayers

Early on in our U-Turn process, my prayers became different because they had to be. For me, it was one continuous prayer: *God, help!* Prayers of desperation are powerful prayers. I was so out of my league trying to lead a U-Turn. I was passionate, but I was desperate. Desperate needs require desperate prayers. I would go off into a forest preserve with my Bible and notebook and read and plead for God to turn the church around. I would read the Bible and get excited about what God could do. I remember reading the book of Acts and praying that it would be our story. Then I would plead with Him: *"O Lord, I know I am not qualified for this job on my own. I know you are sovereign and will do all things for your glory alone, but I am asking, God, please turn this church around! Use me in any way you can to bring new life to your people in this church."*

I prayed almost constantly. I prayed in my car, driving through the neighborhood where I lived. When I went out jogging, I asked the Lord to save the people in each house I passed. Evangelism is as much about prayer as it is about witness. In the end, it is God who saves, but we do the praying and the witnessing.

There is a dynamic that can be described as "speed of the leader, speed of the team" when it comes to prayer. If I wasn't praying, God wasn't working as powerfully as I knew He could. I remember a great line of Bill Hybels that has always stuck with me about prayer: "When we work, we work; when we pray, God works."[1] That is true and powerful for a church that seeks God's renewal. I began to invite our leaders to increase their participation in prayer. I asked our elders, deacons, and close friends to begin an "underground" prayer movement of sorts.

Because I am a high-energy person and wound pretty tightly, I had to adjust my prayer life accordingly. I began praying by myself out loud. With my hands folded and eyes closed, I would often get distracted and start thinking about all the things I had to do, so I began to pray conversationally to God, out loud, eyes open, always trusting that God was listening. The more I prayed, the more fruit I would see in my life, in my leadership, my preaching, and my discipling. James 5:16 states, *"The prayer of a righteous man is powerful and effective."*

Moving Prayer to the Next Level

It was time to move prayer to the next level church-wide. It surprises me how many Christians don't actually pray that much. I know people who came out of the womb loving Jesus, but when you ask them to pray, they freak out. They are willing to talk about the Cubs or the Sox, their grandkids or the weather, but they become silent when you ask them to join you in prayer. Often people don't pray aloud because they think they don't know how. They think it takes a special vernacular or a particular posture, or they just feel that they can't pray acceptably. Christians need to understand the power that is available to them and to their church through prayer. Churches that God renews are churches that have a grass-roots movement of prayer.

Becoming a church that prays happens one soul at a time. It could start with anyone. Maybe there's an elderly woman who had it in her heart to pray faithfully that her church would make a U-Turn to reach the lost. Maybe you already started it. It could start with anybody, but it won't end with everybody until the pastors, elders, deacons, and leaders make prayer a way of life. It moves to every part of the church, to every person in the church. The more people see, hear about, and experience prayer, the more comfortable they will be praying themselves.

In the early days of our U-Turn, I began to expand the prayer movement to a few buddies of mine. I started small with three to five guys. I suggested we get together just to pray. We didn't make a big show or production, we just prayed. It grew in its depth and breadth and power. At times we got up at three AM, met to pray for three hours, and then went out for breakfast. Before you think we were so wonderful, I need to tell you that we were just regular guys. Jesus did it all. I was convicted as I began to write this section because I hadn't done that type of praying in a long time. Last week I was motivated to early morning extended prayer again. Whatever it takes. The bottom line is that we pray.

The next step was to move the prayers to the congregational level. We began to call church-wide days of fasting and prayer for special moments or events that were happening in the church. For example, we called a church-wide day of fasting and prayer leading up to our Christmas Eve services. There was a unity and excitement about what the prayers would cover within our church. We all knew that Christmas Eve was a great door of opportunity for evangelism, because the disconnected often come to Christmas Eve services. God answered our prayers in the numbers of guests who came—something only God could do.

Prayer Ministry

The next step in our U-Turn prayer story was when two women in our church felt called by God to start a formal prayer ministry. One day, one of those women came to me in tears. She said, "I think God is calling me out of the praise team to start a prayer ministry." I knew it was God calling her. Think about it: She was leaving singing, which she loved and did well, to go behind the scenes to start a ministry that she had no clue how to start or what it would look like. She was being called off the platform and onto her knees.

One of the things the women felt was important was a designated place for prayer. They wanted a place that people would know existed where they could go to pray or be prayed for. They created a prayer *room*.

Today the prayer team of Faith Church is about eighty strong, trained people who pray. They pray in various ways, times, and venues. They pray with our people before and after services. They pray in homes and hospitals. They pray with or for staff members personally, on-call, and formally throughout the year. They pray for people who are in crisis, caused a crisis, or are out of a crisis. They sometimes pray during every moment of a weekend service. They come together to pray for the church, the leaders, and current issues. They pray anytime, anyplace. They train other churches how to pray. Along the way we have had our bumps and bruises, maybe even some mountaintops and some valleys. We have had some issues that have had to be addressed, but all in all we are miles ahead from where we were. A prayer ministry is crucial in a U-Turn church.

Unceasing Prayers

Prayer changes people, and a praying people can change a church. Our goal was to become a *church of prayer*. Years ago when I read Paul's letter to the Thessalonica church, it put me in a quandary when Paul asked them to *"pray without ceasing"* (1 Thessalonians 5:17). How do you go through life with your eyes closed? How do you work, pay the bills, and feed the family, if all you're doing is praying? The answer is different, the asking is the same. I believe we pray more than we realize. Usually we equate prayer to specific times and in specific ways. I believe praying without ceasing is to have a nonstop dialogue with God. It is prayer thoughts like "God, thanks for today." When you see the trees budding, you pray, "God, you are awesome." That's a prayer. It's "God, I'm going into this meeting, and I ask that you give me wisdom, insight, Scriptures, and that you keep my mouth shut when I need to, and open it when I should." It's "Lord, bless so-and-so" as you jog or walk past their house. It's the prayer you pray as you pull into the driveway: "Lord, help me to be sensitive to my wife tonight, and help us have fun with the kids." I like to call these prayer thoughts. It's those constant conversational prayers to God that flow from our thoughts.

Other times it will be more formal prayers, or specific prayers, or structured prayers. The goal is to pray all day in your head, out loud, with others, for others, for God's glory. Do I pray without ceasing? Not perfectly, but I pray way more than I used to. Is Faith Church praying without ceasing? Not perfectly, but we pray way more than we used to. Ask me in ten years. I pray it's way more than today. My goal is still to pray a full day without ceasing. As Faith Church strived to pray without ceasing, prayer became the DNA of who we were.

There are different types of prayers I have practiced, and taught about, to encourage a pray-without-ceasing mentality.

Telephone Prayers

I symbolically equate prayers to telephone conversations.

The first type of prayer is the walkie-talkie prayer. Certain cell phones today have walkie-talkie capability in them. Years ago, I had a Nextel cell phone that had this feature. It could be used as a regular cell phone or a walkie-talkie. If someone had a similar phone, we could "walkie-talkie" or "Nextel" each other. These conversations are short and to the point. For example, a boss would chirp an employee: "Hey, it's me, can you pick up two pounds of nails?" Chirp back, "Yep, will do." Prayer can be like that: short chirps to God. A U-Turn church is a church filled with people who are "chirp"-praying all the time.

The second type of prayer is like a regular cell-phone conversation. Most of these conversations are short (unless you're a teenager in love), one to five minutes at best. You call your family, friends, or your clients. You talk about what's going on or what's going to happen. You give quick updates. These are not too intense or too long because there are a lot of things going on around you at the same time. You could be driving or shopping and don't have the time for a long conversation. In the same way, prayers can be offered like a cell-phone conversation to God. One-to-five-minute dialogues, like calling a friend to ask how they're doing. A church that God renews incorporates prayers like that.

The third type of prayer is the long conversational prayer like one you might have on a wall-mount phone. Last week I called a friend, and he said, "Hey, Bob, I want to talk to you. I'll call you back on my land line because I have to talk to you about something important and I don't want to break up or not hear you." He did, and it was a long, clear conversation that lasted almost forty-five minutes. U-Turn churches are filled with people that spend long periods of time alone with God. Praying for long periods requires discipline, structure, and a plan.

ACTS Prayers

One simple and common way to pray is using the ACTS prayer model. This is a great tool to share with the congregation because it will help them have structure to their prayers.

- Adoration—Spend significant time worshiping God.
- Confession—Spend significant time confessing our sins to God.

- Thanksgiving—Offer up a ton of thanks for all the Lord has given and done.
- Supplication—Lay out our needs to the Lord, and pray for others.

Praying through this model makes people ask themselves, "Have I remembered to thank God? Have I remembered to acknowledge how good God is? Have I remembered to confess my sins?" (I don't think anyone ever forgets the supplication part.)

Tabernacle Prayer

Several years ago, I learned the "Tabernacle" pattern of prayer. This has proven to be a very intensive prayer pattern for me and many at Faith Church. This prayer could last fifteen minutes to an hour or more and is very powerful.

I was introduced to this model of prayer about fifteen years ago, when I was asked by our denomination to serve on the board of directors of the National Association of Evangelicals. It was an honor to serve this association with more than fifty other denominations, seeking to influence Washington, DC and Hollywood. We were called to an emergency board meeting in Washington. I don't recall now what the issue was, but I remember the impact it had on my prayer life.

There were about twenty-five of us around the table, and the president of the board told us we were going to hear a special guest greet us and share devotions with us. In walked Dr. David Cho, the pastor of the largest church in the world. At the time, his church had 280,000 members, and now it has over 800,000. He entered the room smiling and very unassuming. In broken English, he began to speak very powerful words about the American Evangelical Christian Church. He said something to the effect: "You Americans have the most amazing church buildings and campuses. Your churches have amazing programs, resources, and publications; however, most American churches are declining or dying. You want to know why? You don't pray." He went on to say, "We Koreans pray!" Then he told us about his prayer life and the prayer life of the people of his church.

The first example of how to become a praying church was his description of their prayer mountain. They literally built a mountain (hill) with a chapel on top solely for prayer. They pray twenty-four hours a day, 365 days a year. Dr. Cho prays there every day at six AM. He shared how one day he overslept and his mother-in-law called and yelled at him. He was there in ten minutes.

The second example he shared, to become a praying church, was the practice of the Tabernacle Prayer model. As I said, it is a prayer pattern that provides a format for an extended time of prayer. I was so inspired by the Tabernacle pattern of prayer that I have been practicing it for fifteen years. Many people in Faith Church practice it as well. This pattern of prayer allows a guide to pray for fifteen minutes, thirty minutes, or an hour or more. I will share an overview of it with you.

Envision the Old Testament tabernacle. The tabernacle was the place to meet and worship God. The people of Israel would go to fellowship, sacrifice, atone for their sins, and worship. There was a flow to the tabernacle. The journey was from far away to the inner Holy of Holies. They, of course, couldn't go into the Holy of Holies; only the high priest was permitted there.

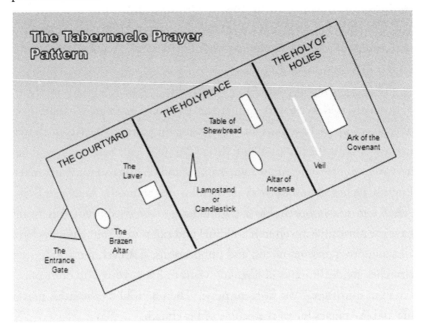

The first section was the *Entrance Gate*. Begin with joy and excitement, knowing that in prayer you are going to meet God. Psalm 100:4 states, *"Enter his gates with thanksgiving . . ."* Begin prayer knowing that Jesus Christ is the way in; Jesus is the entrance gate. Spend moments just celebrating Jesus Christ. Thank Him for being the gate. Thank God that He chose you to enter. He selected you!

Then move past the Entrance Gate into the courtyard. Here are two prayer steps. The first step is the *Brazen Altar*. In Bible times it would be burning, smoky, and smelly. It is here where the sacrifice for sin was made. Focus on Jesus Christ, the full atonement. Focus on the cross, the payment for your sin, forgiveness, and God's grace.

The second step in the courtyard of the tabernacle is the *Laver* or *Basin*. The Basin is filled with water for washing and cleansing. The priest would wash his hands, feet, and face. The water was a mirror where he could see himself. It is here in prayer that you come to the Basin to see yourself in all your sin and to confess and seek to be washed by Jesus' blood and the power of His name. At this point, I will often go through the Ten Commandments, one at a time, and confess how sinful I am and ask for God's forgiveness.

The next section of the Tabernacle Prayer pattern is the *Holy Place*. When you are in communion with Jesus, your complete atonement, and your sins have been washed away, move into the Holy Place. There are three prayer steps within the Holy Place.

The first step is the *Lampstand* or *Candlestick*. It is the symbol of light. It is symbolic of the Holy Spirit's fire. Spend time reflecting upon the light of Christ through the Holy Spirit, and seeking the Holy Spirit's illumination of God's Word in your life and His direction for your ministry. Pray for the fruit of the Spirit and all its manifestations, one by one. Pray for a filling of the Spirit. Pray for the gifts of the Spirit in you and in your church.

The second step is the *Table of Shewbread (Showbread)*. It is a table laid with bread, or manna. It represents the Bread of Life, the Word of God. Spend time thanking God for His Word, claiming its power and promises. Ask the Lord to illumine your eyes to see it more clearly and for God to change you and your church through His Word.

The third step is the *Altar of Incense,* where there is an aroma being lifted up. It is here in prayer that you stop and worship with song or word.

Lift up, as Paul says in 2 Corinthians, *"the aroma of Christ."* [2] Sing a hymn, or listen to your MP3 player in praise and worship. Read a psalm of praise. Seek to join with the angels to worship God and offer an aroma of prayer to the Lord.

The final section of the tabernacle is the *Holy of Holies*. The reason I enjoy this pattern of prayer is because it is a journey, a journey *to* the Holy of Holies. Often I want to jump right to the Holy of Holies, so to speak, where it's me and God and I dump on Him all my needs and concerns. When you pray this pattern, you are in a better place by the time you arrive at the Holy of Holies. It is less about us as individuals and more about God and others.

In the Holy of Holies, imagine yourself at the throne of God. What a privilege. What an honor. Whereas in the Old Testament only the high priest could go into the Holy of Holies once a year, we can enter through Jesus Christ without ceasing. It is in the Holy of Holies where you pray the most intimate prayers for protection for your family, your church family, the larger church family, missions, and God's kingdom to come.

These Tabernacle Prayer times are some of the most intimate times I have with God. I believe it is the place of the biggest kingdom movement in my life and ministry.

Now that you have seen and heard about these prayer patterns, I want you to imagine with me what impact a local church could have through the power of prayer. Jesus, when speaking about the church, said, *"My house will be called a house of prayer."* [3] It's possible. A church that prays, stays. A church that prays makes a U-Turn. A church that prays glorifies God because they know that God has done it all.

Humility and Prayer

Prayer has the power to change us and our churches. The more you pray, the more you realize you need to pray. The less you or your church prays, the less you think you need to pray. Christians need to have an increased awareness of their need for prayer and the need to come to God in humility.

Because of our sinful nature, our personal agendas and selfishness often seep into our prayer life. By utilizing a specific style of prayer, such as ACTS or the Tabernacle Prayer, it will help you keep your focus on God. It says in Psalm 51:10, *"Create in me a pure heart, O God, and renew a steadfast spirit within me."* God alone can purify our motives, and we must ask Him constantly for humility. When we come to God in prayer and with pure motives, there is power.

The more Faith Church grew as a church in heartfelt prayer, the more we were able to die to ourselves, our agendas, our plans, and our thoughts, and the more our agendas, plans, and thoughts became those of God. God's Word says: *"[God] gives good gifts to those who ask him!"*[4] When your agenda becomes God's agenda, what you ask for changes. God is filled with blessings, awaiting your request. The Bible reminds us, *"You do not have, because you do not ask God."*[5] When was the last time as a church or as an individual you asked God for converts? I believe it is the Holy Spirit that leads people to Christ, converts them, and fills them with His Holy Spirit. Why wouldn't we ask for that in prayer? When a church prays for salvation, they become more alert to opportunities to witness or invite people to worship. When we're praying with a pure heart, God is leading, directing, aligning, and revealing His will for us and His church.

God uses a humble, praying church for His kingdom advancement as a whole as well as for us personally. Praying humbly changes the heart of the pray-er. It moves and changes the soul of the person who prays. It makes Christians think about God more often and God's agenda rather than what we want from God in our own personal lives. It moves the church to be more dependent upon God. The best possible posture for a U-Turn is humility and prayer. God blesses a church that is filled with humble, pure, submitted Christians who pray without ceasing.

Prayer Stokes the Fire

Holy zeal is the fuel that keeps the fire burning; prayer is the tool used to stoke the fire. Part of the process of a U-Turn church can only happen through prayer. There are some very deep things that have to transpire that a program or a good sermon can't accomplish. In Mark 9, the disciples were trying to turn a person around by performing a miracle. They said to Jesus, "What's up? Why can't we do this?" Jesus said, *"This kind can come out only through prayer."* [6] The same is true for us. Some things can only happen through prayer.

I remember a point in the U-Turn process when I was being pretty beat up by some people that were upset by the changes required. It was a low time in my soul. About three AM I got up to pray. I went into the family room and knelt on the floor with my elbows on the La-Z-Boy and prayed. I poured out my heart to God. I begged Him, pleaded with Him, to give me and our leaders wisdom. I didn't hear a voice. I didn't experience any unique manifestations of God, but I sensed His presence. In my heart, God gave me the confidence and the joy I needed to carry on. He granted us decision-making capability that was laser sharp. I can tell when my prayer life is on track. I can tell when our church's prayer life is on track by the wisdom that God grants us and the confidence to make the big decisions.

Five hundred years ago, John Calvin, when speaking about prayer, spoke about the "fire that happens when we pray." He spoke about the source behind the prayers that can turn anything around, the power of God's Holy Spirit. He wrote, "The meaning rather is that when the faithful feel cold and sluggish or somewhat indisposed to pray, they should forthwith flee to God and demand that they be inflamed with the fiery darts of His Spirit, so as to be rendered fit for prayer."[7]

Churches need to be inflamed! Churches that desire to see themselves turned around need the fiery darts that Calvin spoke of to be rendered fit to pray. If you don't feel like praying, pray that God would inflame you with the fiery darts of His Spirit.

Boiler Room Prayers

As I close this chapter, I need to tell you about the boiler room prayers. In the early part of our U-Turn, God turned us around from a church *that prayed* to a church *of prayer,* and we were growing. We ran out of room at our old facility. On Wednesday night worship services, the church was packed and fully utilized. It was one of those Wednesday nights that my prayer buddies and I wanted to pray and there was no place to pray. The sanctuary was full. Sunday school rooms were all taken. There was literally no place to pray, so someone suggested the boiler room. There had to be eight or more furnaces and air-conditioning units in the room. We would gather in the center, where there was an empty space. There were no chairs of course, and we would get down on our knees to pray. It was noisy, it was aesthetically ugly, it was amongst the brooms, the mops, the tools, but it became our Holy of Holies, where God worked. Today, we have a new facility, larger, more beautiful. We have a prayer room now too, but there's a part of me that misses the boiler room, where God heard us and met us and turned us around. How ironic that one of the most intimate, powerful times, when God stoked the fire in our hearts through our prayers, happened in the midst of the fiery furnaces in the boiler room of our church.

Kevin's Reflections on Prayer

For Corinth Church, the genesis of the U-Turn came in a parking lot, living rooms, and in hearts all over the community. Emma Jerene walked around the church parking lot praying for God to come and do something mighty at Corinth Church for the sake of Jesus. She did this for years. Grandma Lois, Katherine, Dorothy, Fred and Annie, and a team of other faithful saints had been praying for Corinth Reformed Church to become a city on a hill. They longed for the love, message, and light of Jesus to fill the community.

For many years, passionate Christ followers spent time on their knees, asking God to do something through this little country church that would bring honor to Jesus, bless the community, and grow the believers in the church. They did not use the term *U-Turn* in their prayers. They prayed for revival! They asked God for a visitation. They wanted to see a movement of renewal. As they prayed, they dared to ask the God of heaven to invade this small patch of earth in Byron Center, Michigan, and do something glorious in their midst.

All of these humble prayer warriors got to see the beginning of the U-Turn up close and personal. Some of them continue to watch from the glory of heaven as they have joined that great cloud of witnesses and cheer on those who have come after them.[8]

One aspect of the prayer ministry of Corinth I would like to add to the great lessons Bob brings to this chapter is this: God raised up a prayer team to surround the pastors of Corinth Church and their families. For *every single day* of my thirteen years of ministry at Corinth there was a team of tenacious prayer warriors who prayed a hedge of protection around me, Sherry, and our three boys. As the pastoral team grew, they prayed for the rest of our leaders. Many of these people would tell us, "I pray for you every day!" Even though I now live on the West Coast, I still get calls and letters assuring me that these mighty prayer warriors intercede for each of my family members every day. What a comfort.

We knew this was true at the time.

In some of the tough times along the way, I felt those prayers. When the enemy would seek to attack us, it was the intercessions of these mighty women and men of God that fortified and protected us. I am convinced that someday, when I am in glory, God will pull back the veil and show me how many countless times we were protected by the prayers of these mighty brothers and sisters.

If you are at the very beginning of the U-Turn journey in your church, pray with passion and fervor. Pray for revival, for renewal, and for a U-Turn that will bring glory to God. If you are already on your way, would you consider praying for your pastors and leaders every day? Making a U-Turn in a church is serious business, and the forces of hell will rise up against those who lead and work and pray. Fortify your leaders with prayer. Ask the Lord of glory to protect your church leaders. Cry out to the Holy Spirit to fill your pastor to overflowing. Pray to the sovereign God of the universe and ask Him to hold your leaders firmly in His hand.

Enter the work of ministry and the battle in the heavenly realms and pray for God's will in your church. Your prayers have more power than you dream or imagine!

U-Turn Exercises and Activities

Action Steps for Church Leaders

- Consider creating a prayer room at your church. Unleash someone's creative interior design talent and let them make a space that is aesthetically peaceful, comfortable, inviting, and welcoming for people to pray and to be prayed for.

- Consider establishing a prayer team. Find a few people who have the gift of intercession, who are willing to follow biblical and theological guidelines, have a humble spirit of submission to the elders of the church, and set them free to pray.

- Consider calling a church-wide day of fasting and prayer leading up to a special event, sermon series, or holiday outreach. Also consider breaking the fast together with a meal.

- Consider inviting your congregation to a special night where a teacher takes them through the Tabernacle Prayer model, and then break off in small groups to practice it.

U-Turn Prayers

- Take an honest inventory of your prayer life over the past month or months. How often have you prayed? And when you pray, consider what percentage of your prayer requests are for the church and what percentage for the lost in your area. Consider a tithe, a percentage of your prayers for the expansion of God's kingdom.

- Suggested Prayer:

  Father in heaven, we confess to you that we don't pray as we ought. Ignite our hearts with the fiery darts of your Spirit to enable us to pray. Create in us a life of unceasing prayer. Stoke the fire of prayer in our church to a new intensity so that we are changed, as well as the people around us. Jesus, we lift up your name; we plead with you to draw people to yourself. Turn our church around for your glory, now and forevermore! In Jesus' name. Amen.

Section Two

The Middle of the U-Turn

Holy zeal, urgency, vision, and prayer . . . these are the beginnings of a U-Turn. Without these, no amount of strategy or planning will get the job done. A U-Turn is a work of God, not the fabrication of people. If your church is praying, passionate for souls, focused on the vision of God, and feeling the urgency of the Holy Spirit, you are ready to move forward.

The middle of the U-Turn journey is a glorious place to be. It is a place of adventure and trust in God. It is the season when we begin to ask new and dynamic questions:

- What do we really believe with such conviction that we would die for it?
- Why do we have a church board or leadership team, and what are they supposed to be doing?
- What does God expect of a person who claims to follow Jesus and is a member or regular attendee of our church?
- How can we stay tender in heart but still press forward when some of our members are actively resisting the work of God in our midst?

- Are we willing to take serious risks for the sake of Jesus and His gospel?
- How can we reach beyond our church walls to love our community and those who have not yet discovered God's grace?
- How can we "do church" in a way that will connect with people who are far from Jesus?

These questions, and others like them, will propel a local church forward on a U-Turn journey.

5

Biblical Truths vs. Personal Preferences

by Bob Bouwer

Sometimes our personal preferences line up with the truth and teaching of the Bible . . . a surprising amount of the time, they do not.

A crucial mile marker in the U-Turn church experience is to qualify the differences between what the Bible says are biblical absolutes and people's personal preferences. God gave the Church a mission to disciple people and to make itself attractive to those outside the local church. God offers us direction along the way. Often churches make their route to this destination a biblical absolute, when in reality there are different routes to the same destination. God knows the best route for your church. As we seek God for direction, we realize that we need to make a U-Turn from some of the roads that have distracted us from the mission of God.

When a church is making a U-Turn, some degree of change is required, and change can be difficult. People become upset and experience all kinds of emotions that they might not identify as fear or sadness. The familiar roads that they have traveled are being replaced with new roads in unfamiliar territory.

The Dry-Erase Board

Part of the way we dealt with those who were struggling with change was to get them together to process what they were going through. As senior pastor, a lead elder and I personally invited to a meeting in the church library people who we knew were having a tough time with all that was happening. As I recall, there were twenty-five to thirty adults, most of them in their mid-fifties at the time. I opened the meeting with prayer and then I handed the platform over to the elder. This was an important move because now a layperson was speaking to laypeople. He went to the dry-erase board mounted on the wall, and began: "We are aware that some of you are upset about the changes that are taking place at Faith Church, and I am going to write down on this board the things that seem to be most upsetting for you."

He began listing them: "We no longer use choir robes. We no longer have a choir loft. We're not using the hymnals. Pastor Bob's not wearing a suit. There are drums in the church. We don't know everyone's name. The music is too loud. We're not using the organ. We don't like to see the words on a screen. We don't like the way some people dress in church." There were about twenty complaints on the board when he finished writing.

Then the elder stepped to the other side of the board and made a *T*, forming two columns. "Now let's take these issues and place them under one of two categories: Bible Absolutes and Personal Preferences." One by one he mentioned each issue and asked whether it fell under biblical absolutes or personal preferences. As you can imagine, every single complaint ended up on the side of personal preferences.

We didn't do this to rub it in their faces, but to graciously explain to them that the route may be changing but our destination had not. We emphasized the fact that we would never intentionally do *anything* at Faith Church that is unbiblical. And if we did do something unbiblical and it was pointed out to us, we would repent of it. We asked them to try to understand that what they were dealing with were personal preferences. We also explained why we made the decisions we made concerning these issues.

I can't say that everything was rosy after that meeting. But the exercise was a good starting point for discussion and it gave birth to great movement forward. Almost all the people in that room stayed through the changes and are still part of Faith Church today. A few left, but on good terms.

Defining Biblical Absolutes

As leaders we reflected on that experience and discovered the importance of identifying personal preferences and biblical absolutes. You cannot fudge on biblical absolutes. The Bible teaches that worship is to include prayer, teaching and preaching of the Word, offerings, songs of praises, sacraments, fellowship, and church discipline. None of these are up for debate.

I shared 1 Timothy 4:16 with the Faith Church staff: *"Watch your life and doctrine closely. Persevere in them, because if you do, you will save both yourself and your hearers."* We must watch our doctrine closely so that we do not let sin distort the true Word of God. The virgin birth, the authority of Scripture, the resurrection of Jesus Christ, salvation through Christ alone, the Ten Commandments, loving one another—these are biblical absolutes.

Biblical Convictions

In reality, there is a third category that falls between biblical absolutes and personal preferences. It's called biblical convictions. These have biblical support but are often grounds for disagreement among Christians.

For example, infant baptism is one of these. The Bible says, "Repent and be baptized." What often causes disagreement among us is infant baptism versus adult baptism. At Faith Church, we baptize infants because we believe it is a symbol of God's covenant with us. We see the connection between the Old Testament practice of circumcision and the New Testament practice of baptism. I am sometimes asked by members why we don't wait to baptize until someone is an adult and can make their own decision. I answer them that we have the biblical conviction at Faith Church that the whole of Scripture (Old and New Testaments) communicates God's initiative from generation to generation. Personal preference with regard to baptism often involves the amount of water used: sprinkling or pouring versus full immersion. These personal preferences do not change the meaning and symbolism of baptism as God's covenant with us.

As we went through the changes at Faith Church, I didn't have this third category (biblical convictions) to consider, but if I led the change today, I would use all three categories and seek to bring clarification and communication through them.

Wet Cement

Biblical truths are absolute, but personal preferences are what we at Faith Church call "wet cement." What this means is that we need to be careful that we don't make things that could be moved around hard and fast rules. We have flexibility in those areas. In high school and college, I worked for a concrete company in Wisconsin. We would pour concrete for basement walls and floors, and garage floors. The guys and I *loved* playing with the wet cement. If one of our co-workers would leave for lunch, we would take his boots and place them in the concrete that he'd just poured. He'd come back and find his boots in the middle of the garage floor, and we all had a good laugh. We would write our names in the wet cement, or words like *Hi*, using rebar pieces. Because the concrete wasn't set yet, we could have fun and still smooth it out before it hardened.

Understanding that some things are flexible is part of the U-Turn process. What the church has to say to the world is that God is calling us to a relationship with himself. This relationship, broken by sin, can be restored in the person of Jesus Christ through the forgiveness of our sins and through faith in Christ. That is *what* we must communicate to the world, but *how* we communicate it is more or less up for grabs. We try to creatively communicate the gospel of Jesus Christ. And that creativity will always be flexible. Something that worked at one time may not work in a few years.

Traditionalism

Part of the process of making a U-Turn is that people have to realize that many of the rituals and traditions of a church fall in the category of personal preferences. We need to learn the difference between biblical absolutes and personal preferences. When you treat personal preferences as if they were biblical absolutes, you can create a stumbling block in the church. There are traditions in the church that *are* biblical absolutes, but many of them are personal preferences. In Matthew 15:1–3, Jesus addresses this issue of traditionalism:

> *Then some Pharisees and teachers of the law came to Jesus from Jerusalem and asked, "Why do your disciples break the tradition of the elders? They don't wash their hands before they eat!" Jesus replied, "And why do you break the command of God for the sake of your tradition?"*

This account is also told in the book of Mark, where Jesus responded: *"You have let go of the commands of God and are holding on to the traditions of men"* (7:8).

This is not saying that everyone who holds to traditional church services disobeys the Bible; the point that Jesus is making is that it is more important to obey the Bible than to obey traditions made by man.

The Word of God is absolute, and it trumps all our thoughts, all our feelings, all our traditions, all our rituals, and all our practices in what church is about.

The Devil's Rhythm?

Toward the beginning of our U-Turn, I had an interesting experience with one of our elders. This godly man, now in his nineties, has been and is a great supporter of our church and a supporter of me as pastor. He was always encouraging to me, but one thing that bugged him was the use of drums in our church. Almost every weekend he would say to me, "Great job—the service was great, but I can't stand those drums." At one point he told me that he read an article that said that drums are of the devil and there are certain beats that are the devil's rhythm, and he believed that.

I said to him, "Okay, I usually have Mondays off, but I want to meet with you for coffee at the local coffee shop. I have just one requirement:

I want you to bring your Bible." He said, "Okay." We got there and I had my Bible and he had his Bible, and we sat down at the table. I said, "We're going to play a little Bible search game. I'm going to look up all the verses that have the word *piano* and *organ* in them, and you look up the verses that have anything to do with percussion and drums and rhythm, and the one who finds the most verses, wins."

He looked up at me and smiled and said, "You got me."

I said, "Do you know what? I'm not trying to get you." And I went on to tell him that the Bible always trumps our personal preferences. And the Bible *does* speak of rhythm and the Bible *does* speak about worshiping the Lord with drums; the Bible *does* speak about worshiping the Lord with percussion instruments. Every good and perfect gift is from God, the Scriptures tell us.[1] But to say that drums should not be in a worship service and make the piano and organ absolutes is not biblically based. Not that there's anything wrong with people's preferences, but they are just that—personal preferences. It is biblical to incorporate music into our worship, but the style of music we choose to use is a personal preference.

Part of the U-Turn experience is to understand the areas that are personal preferences and to release them if necessary for the sake of the gospel. We must be willing to die to our own personal preferences while always upholding the ultimate authority of God's truth found in His Word.

By processing with people and clarifying their personal preferences, the deeper issues are uncovered. The underlying issues of loss and fear are greater than the issues people are against. They are afraid that their church is cutting off everything from their past. They are afraid that they will no longer be able to sing their favorite hymns. Ultimately, the root is the fear of being out of control in this area of their life. It is no longer safe. Once the fears were uncovered, people were able to deal with them. They were comforted knowing that the church would not continue in or pursue any unbiblical direction. They were also comforted that there would be new ways to incorporate their hymns.

Examples of Biblical Absolutes vs. Personal Preferences

We've already briefly touched on some examples of personal prefer-ences and biblical truths, but let's examine a few examples in more detail. This won't be an exhaustive list, but it will give you an idea of issues that churches wrestle with.

Music Style of Worship

Scriptures instruct us to *"Sing praises to the Lord,"* [2] *"make music to [his] name,"* [3] and *"extol him with music and song."* [4] It is biblical that music be incorporated into worship. Even without any instruments at all, the Lord will put a song in our mouth.[5] Moses and the Israelites sang a song to the Lord with the lyrics: *"The Lord is my strength and my song"* (Exodus 15:2), emphasizing that the point of using music in worship is to bring our entire focus on the Lord. The Lord is our song. The rhythm, the instruments, and the style we use to worship the Lord are personal preferences.

I'm fascinated by the fact that two-thirds of all the Christians in the world worship with instruments other than the piano or organ. Because American churches were highly influenced by Western Europe, our worship is as it is. This is not wrong. Again, it is a personal preference or a tradition. Yet when churches attempt to change the music style and instruments used in churches, people tend to react as if it were a biblical absolute. In reality, the organ style of worship is in the minority compared to the global wor-ship style. Although your church in general may prefer to worship using the organ and hymnbooks, if you ask people in your community what their preference is, you will likely find what we discovered when we surveyed the surrounding towns. We found that many prefer a band over the organ, the song words on a screen rather than in a hymnbook, and the style of music they're used to listening to. I encourage you to survey the community around your church if you are interested in reaching out to those around you.

Church Décor and Personal Attire

The Bible teaches that the true Church is the believing people, not a building. We have been asked by many why we don't have crosses, stained-glass windows, or other symbols in our church. Symbolism may enhance one person's worship experience, but could encourage idolatry for another. Scripture does not say whether or not we are to use symbolism in the church, but it does forbid idolatry. *"God is spirit, and his worshipers must worship in spirit and in truth"* (John 4:24). Faith Church is intentional in having symbolism occasionally but not permanently, because we want to communicate that it is more important for an individual to enter into a relationship with God than enter into a religious-looking building.

Just because it's a personal preference does not mean it's right or wrong. Having a cross in the church is a meaningful symbol, but my personal preference would be to have a cross displayed just half the weekends in a year. This would show that it is a legitimate symbolic preference, but would discourage undue ritual or even idolatry. Not having a cross up permanently would also discourage taking the powerful symbolism for granted. If a cross is on stage up front every single week, people stop seeing it.

Style of dress is another personal preference. If you were raised in the church, you probably are aware that there was an unwritten rule as to what you had to wear to church. You were expected to wear your "Sunday best"; it was a big deal. Let's talk about that in terms of biblical example. What did Jesus wear? He didn't wear the high priestly robes; He wore common people's clothing. Does Scripture instruct us how to dress? The Bible says this:

> *I also want women to dress modestly, with decency and propriety, not with braided hair or gold or pearls or expensive clothes, but with good deeds, appropriate for women who profess to worship God.*
> (1 Timothy 2:9–10)

In the survey that we took in our community, we discovered that worry over dressing up made the top three on the list of reasons why people no longer go to church. Scripture says *"not with . . . gold or pearls or expensive clothes,"* yet unchurched people don't want to go to church *because* they feel they have to have *"gold or pearls or expensive clothes."* How backward the church's stereotypes have become.

I remember one time an elder, in our transformational years of turning around, expressed his concern at an elders' meeting because a young man was coming to church with blue hair and wearing a baseball cap through the entire service. Before addressing his concern, I thought to myself, "Praise God! He's coming to church!" A woman wearing braids in the New Testament time was known to be promiscuous. Yet a woman wearing braids in today's society is the exact opposite; it represents innocence, commonly worn by little girls. Our culture is constantly changing, and we must be aware of what that means. A man takes his hat off in church because it represents respect. A WWII veteran knows the underwritten code that you took your hat off when you came into the house, especially the house of the Lord, as they used to say. Are we to pull aside an innocent attendee during a service and require that person to obey a man-made rule?

Faith Church decided that we would be prepared to address attire issues only if they were clearly going against God's instructions to remain modest. Of course, the definition of modesty is different for different people, but there are obvious indecencies that every person would agree are definitely not modest. With all the thousands of people that walk through our doors week after week, we have never had to pull someone aside and say that they were not welcome to worship because of how they were dressed. We have people come in baseball uniforms on their way to a game and we have people come from work in uniforms. We've seen a lot of different attire, but people are smart. They know that there are certain ways of dressing that across the board are inappropriate for church.

Volunteers and staff have modeled what is appropriate. We discuss with those going on the platform to be conscious of how their appearance might be perceived. Occasionally, we have had to address issues with a person's attire that he or she may not have been aware of. The people up front are setting an example for the congregation, and the volunteers and staff must be made aware of that and held accountable.

Education

What is the biblical absolute about the training of a pastor, an elder, a deacon, or any other leader in the church? In the Bible, you'll never find the word *college,* or the word *seminary.* You'll never find the word *ordination* either, but in some respects I wrestle with defining this as a biblical truth or a personal preference. I think seminaries are outstanding, especially if they're solid in the Word of God, and from my perspective, the reformed understanding of theology. I am a graduate from seminary. I believe training is necessary, vital. But to hold the training of our leaders to seminary, whether it's distance learning or a three-year resident program, is not a biblical mandate.

A great model is Jesus Christ, who said, "Walk with me." He selected twelve disciples and trained them himself. We have campus pastors with different educational training, including on-site seminary, distance learning seminary, and the commissioning pastor program, which is outside seminary training offered by our denomination. A few were trained and educated before they came on staff at Faith Church. A few were trained while they were on staff. The point is, education is important and biblical, but how that is achieved, I believe, is a preference.

Church Government

What are the biblical mandates of church government? Looking at Scripture, we see elders and deacons. The call of elders is to oversee and the call of deacons is to be stewards of our resources and to assist widows, orphans, and the poor.

In our denomination, the Reformed Church of America, we have a Presbyterian form of government. This means the elders and deacons together make up a board called the consistory, and that's where the authority for the church rests. I think it's a great model. But sometimes this structure limits the capability of a local church. For example, when I first came to Faith Church, we had committees overseeing certain ministries. The nursery committee, made up of about six women, wanted to improve the nursery space. After evaluating the nursery, they came up with a wish list of items, including new carpet with thick padding beneath for the sake of the children who are crawling on it all the time, a better color scheme, some new equipment, and new furniture. In short, they wanted to overhaul the nursery. If I recall correctly, it would have cost about $6,000 in the mid-

1990s. They made a recommendation to our consistory, and my heart broke because the consistory, generally made up of older men that didn't have little children, saw the price tag of $6,000 and said *no*. They didn't have the passion for little children that these women did. They didn't see the value of investing in the nursery, and they voted it down. It destroyed much of the momentum in that group, because to them they were being told their ministry wasn't valued much. The message was, "We're in charge, and we'll make that decision."

Part of our U-Turn process involved our church government. I suggested to the consistory that we reverse it. Let's get rid of the word *committee* and change it to *team*. And what if, instead of seeing ourselves as the gatekeepers and police, we *trust* that team? Let's give them a budget, let's give them authority, and tell them they are the overseers of that space and we trust them. The only thing we will do is oversee the teams and be there for them. If we see a team do anything that is unbiblical, we will address it. If we see a team do something unwise, like using up their entire budget in the first month of the year, we'll discuss it. Ever since we incorporated those changes, we saw the blessing. Teams felt responsible, valued, and trusted. Instead of having to ask people to be on a committee, people desired to be on teams and came forward on their own. It was transformational for Faith Church.

When I looked at our church government as a whole, I realized that we stumbled onto something big and that this could work at a higher level. I asked our leaders if this was actually working as well as it could. We all agreed that the answer was no. We began restructuring our top level of church government.

We still have a consistory made up of elders and deacons, but we formed a management team made up of men and women who make decisions week to week. The Management Team is under the authority of the consistory, but they make decisions without having to bring it to the consistory. This streamlines our day-to-day decision making and allows the consistory to focus on bigger issues.

That being said, we realized our consistory didn't have the time to concentrate on our future as we felt was necessary, so we created the Vision

Team. This team's function is to wrestle, pray, and ask the Lord where we are to go next.

The Vision Team has the biblical authority of elders and deacons, but with this restructuring we have become more efficient by making better use of people's gifts and time.

Tips for Those Who Are Wrestling With Biblical Truths vs. Personal Preferences

Handle With Care

The first tip is to make sure that the process of defining biblical truths and personal preferences is handled with grace. *"Let your conversation be always full of grace, seasoned with salt, so that you may know how to answer everyone"* (Colossians 4:6). The Bible says that whatever you do and say, do it all for the glory of God. The Bible talks about character. Often when churches are battling between biblical truths and personal preferences, people use non-Christian behavior when discussing these topics. In other words, they sin. They will get angry, they will shout and scream, and even use language inappropriate in any setting. I believe the key here is grace and humility.

There were a couple of times when I blew it. One time a man was in our narthex complaining about our music and how loud it was. His complaining was heard clearly by those around him, and he was an elder in our church. I lacked grace and I blew it. I walked up to him in front of all of his friends and said, "The reason we are doing this is because we want to reach your son." His adult son was in his twenties and had left the church. Later, I went back and apologized to him. I confessed to him that I should not have done what I did. I should have pulled him aside. I should have used the Matthew 18 principle and talked to him alone. If that didn't work, I was to bring an eyewitness with me. I was out of bounds.

I want you to learn from my mistakes and remember that it is supremely important to the process of making a U-Turn to be sure your conversation is always abounding in grace, humility, and unconditional love. I am happy to say that restoration has been made with that man and their son is also back and fully engaged in the church.

Avoid Avoiding

A second tip is not to avoid going into the topics that are difficult. Early in our U-Turn process, I found it easier to avoid the people I knew were talking about me. I knew there was an elder in the church who every time he greeted me was nice and friendly, but people in his small group told me how mad he was at me and at the church. Instead of talking to him I would avoid him, and he avoided me. That was inappropriate and it was wrong. It encouraged resentment and bitterness. Through our U-Turn process, I have learned the better way of addressing a problem. Part of the beauty of a U-Turn is to go into the alleys that are difficult with the Bible in one hand and the character of Christ in the other and say, "Let's talk."

Hear People

Another tip is to experiment with the type of meeting that I spoke about earlier in the chapter where we used a dry-erase board. Invite people that have concerns into a meeting and fill it with a lot of prayer and grace. Tell them that you want them to have an opportunity to be heard. Establish boundaries before your meeting starts (such as you're not going to throw things or use words that are inappropriate). Ask them to be specific with the things they're concerned about. In this process you may discover that some of their stuff is personal preference, but assure them that whatever is biblically absolute you will always hold to.

Dangers of Flags in the Sand

The last tip is to be careful about putting "flags in the sand," a phrase implying that once you put your flag in the sand, you're standing by it. I encourage churches to be careful about this because they may even begin to see that they are wrong about something, but since they've already put their flag in the sand, they feel they would be reneging if they took it back. Often people will put a flag in the sand for something that is merely a personal preference, and once they put it there, too much is at stake to remove it.

I will always stand by the authority of Scripture, the virgin birth, the Trinity, the bodily resurrection of Jesus Christ, and all other biblical absolutes. But I will not put my flag in the sand over a personal preference.

Reformed and Always Reforming

I want to conclude by sharing a beautiful phrase that we hold to in our tradition. We are a Reformed Church, so that means our theology goes back to the Reformation of the 1500s. It means that we go back to the Apostle's Creed, the Heidelberg Catechism, and the Canons of Dort. We are also called Calvinists. The phrase that I heard in college was that we are *reformed and always reforming*. I love that.

Now what does that mean? It means that our tradition is Reformed but we're always going to be reforming according to the Word of God. So yes, styles and preferences and cultural things will always change. But the Word of God remains the same. It's a beautiful thing. We should remind churches that there are always things that will be changing, but the Word of God will never change.

Kevin's Reflections on Biblical Truths vs. Personal Preferences

Same battles, same questions, same stories. What Bob experienced in a suburb of Chicago, we walked through in the cornfields of Bryon Center. I was not as clever as Bob when it came to putting things up on a board for everyone to see. I love that story and the whole process of being clear about what is a biblical absolute and what is simply our personal likes and preferences. I commend the idea to you wholeheartedly and wish I had used it early in our U-Turn process. It would have saved me lots of time and many challenges.

Our approach was to deal with things issue-by-issue. When we decided to introduce drums into our worship experience, I read from Psalm 150 and reminded everyone that God calls us to use percussion instruments when we sing. If they had a problem with drums, their issue was with God, not me. Surprisingly, almost everyone got it! Even though we tried new ways to do worship and various styles of music, as long as we were clear that God's Word affirms new things, people really tried to embrace it. When people would say, "But I like the old music," I would listen and seek to be caring and pastoral. I also reminded them that the Bible calls us to "sing a new song."[6] It never says, "sing an old song." This does not mean old songs are bad, but it does call us to explore new songs and music.

When we faced systemic issues that came from our church government and traditions, we would go to the Word of God and make sure we were not committing idolatry by making sacred cows out of human systems. If it was not a biblical truth, we decided that we would not be bound by past systems and patterns. Of course, there were people who pushed back and did not like trying new things. But I reminded myself that these were people who really loved God and believed in His Word. We would give them a chance to argue their case from Scripture. If it became clear that the real issue was their personal preference, we would name it and move on. This freed people to express their likes and dislikes, while freeing the church to try new things . . . as long as they were not contrary to Scripture.

Now, over sixteen years into the U-Turn process, Corinth Church still asks the basic questions: Is this a biblical teaching or mandate? Or is this just about our personal likes and tastes? What the church has learned is that there is no way we will ever satisfy all the tastes of everyone in the church. Our first concern always needs to be staying under the teaching of God's Word.

U-Turn Exercises and Activities

Action Steps for Church Leaders

1. If you have already begun the U-Turn process and are experiencing unhappy people, write down the names of people that you could potentially invite to a meeting to listen to their concerns.

2. Regardless of where you are in the U-Turn process, meet with a core group of leaders to define some of the personal preferences in your church.

3. Consider doing an internal survey. Listed below are some questions that are on our internal survey.
    1. What would you say are the three things your church does best?
       (a)

       (b)

       (c)

    2. If you were asked the purpose of your church, how would you answer?
    3. I would say my church's ministries and programs are helping to achieve our purpose:
       Strongly Agree | Agree | Neutral | Disagree | Strongly Disagree
       If you answered Disagree or Strongly Disagree, please explain.
    4. What are three ways you would like to see your church making an impact for the kingdom of God?

5. I am comfortable inviting my friends, family, and co-workers to worship with me at my church:
   Strongly Agree | Agree | Neutral | Disagree | Strongly Disagree
   Please explain.

6. List three areas we could focus on improving in our church:
   (a)

   (b)

   (c)

   Do you have suggestions for making these improvements?

7. My church provides quality opportunities for people to connect with others in the church:
   Strongly Agree | Agree | Neutral | Disagree | Strongly Disagree
   If you answered Disagree or Strongly Disagree, please explain.

8. My church provides quality opportunities to be discipled:
   Strongly Agree | Agree | Neutral | Disagree | Strongly Disagree
   If you answered Disagree or Strongly Disagree, please let us know what discipleship opportunities would be beneficial for you.

9. Please add any other information you think would be important for the Vision Team/Consistory board to know.

6

Unleashing Leaders

by Kevin G. Harney

*Some of the best resources for a dynamic U-Turn are free, plentiful,
and already sitting right in your church!*

Susan was not a complainer.

She was a gifted leader in the marketplace, the community, and the local church. She had an amazing servant's heart. This is why I was surprised and shocked with what she said when she came to meet with me. Susan expressed, with genuine sadness, that she was seriously considering leaving Corinth Church.

I knew she loved the people, enjoyed the preaching and worship, was relationally connected, and engaged in ministry. When I asked what was leading her toward this decision, she explained that she wanted to invest in the church *on a more significant level.* She wanted to use her gifts in a way that would make a difference for the kingdom of God.

I knew she had made herself available to serve at deeper levels at Corinth, but no one had pulled her in and leveraged her gifts. Here was a talented leader who was considering leaving the church not because we were asking too much, but because she wanted to do more!

The truth is, we were still early in the U-Turn process and had not yet established strategic ways of engaging, training, and deploying people in ministry. Specifically, we had not taken great strides to help leaders find their place in ministry on a level that would bear fruit for God and bring them the deep joy of serving in substantial ways.

In that moment, I was confronted with the sobering reality that unleashing leaders for ministry had to be a higher priority if we were going to continue moving forward in our U-Turn process.

Over the coming decade, we worked hard to identify the roadblocks that were standing in the way of our identifying, equipping, and unleashing leaders for God's kingdom. What follows is not a specific road map that will tell you exactly what to do. The truth is, transforming a church leadership culture is not that simple.

What I can share is that we spent a lot of time identifying obstacles and found ways to get past them. My hope is that reading about our journey will help you identify similar roadblocks to developing leaders in your ministry context and find your way around, over, or through them.

Roadblock #1: An Unhealthy Understanding of Leadership

Pre-U-Turn Snapshot

For one hundred years, Corinth Church functioned with a very specific model of ministry and leadership. It was the way most churches worked back then, and sadly, many still function today. In simple terms, it was a clergy-centered leadership model. They hired a pastor to do the work of ministry. Most of the church members saw themselves as the recipients of ministry. The pastor was the one who did the actual ministry, that's why they called him the *Minister*.

Leadership in the "important things" was reserved for trained professionals. Sure, church members could help in the nursery, teach a Sunday school class, set up chairs, and even be on the church board, but the important stuff was done by clergy.

Early on, I saw a number of telltale signs that the church was still in a clergy-centered mentality. One was that many people in the church expected the pastor to come and call on them when they were in the hospital, sick, or struggling. If someone else came, they would say things like, "No one came to visit me!" The truth was, a number of their friends came, an elder came, and maybe a small-group leader dropped in, but they still felt free to announce, "No one came to see me." This was code for, "The guy who stands up and preaches on Sunday did not come and meet my needs." Or, "The real minister never showed up."

Another sign was when I began to recruit leaders to grow the outreach ministry. I had people make subtle comments like "Isn't that what we pay you for?" and "If we do the outreach what are *you* going to do?" This was a clear indicator that they still saw the pastor as the primary dispenser of ministry.

A third and more subtle sign was that people in the church looked to me to give them permission to do things rather than taking the initiative and moving out in service. There was an unspoken understanding that people were supposed to wait to do ministry until I gave some kind of formal blessing. In addition, the church board needed to sign off and affirm any new initiative. This mindset was confining and blocked the flow of new ideas, innovation, and ministry strategies.

U-Turn Philosophy and Action

Our leadership U-Turn began to gain momentum as I communicated a new vision and philosophy of leadership. In the past, these words were printed in the bulletin each week:

Minister . . . Rev. Jonathan Vander, Pastor

We changed it to say:

Ministers . . . All who follow Jesus

This became a symbol of what we taught and reinforced over and over for the coming years. It was not a simple tweak in verbiage. It became a philosophy of life and ministry for the church.

I preached a message early on, titled, "The Ministers Are Not Doing Their Job!" We looked at the vision clearly taught in Ephesians 4:11–12 that says pastors and teachers are called to *"prepare God's people for works of service."* Also, the church board studied the biblical passages that make it clear that the church is a priesthood of all believers.[1]

At the same time we started our U-Turn process, I was just finishing a doctoral program focused on one primary idea: How we build the church around the gifts of all God's people (the true ministers and God's holy priesthood), and not on the charisma and skills of a pastor. In the coming years, we explored any and every way to move the ministry from the pastor to the congregation. In doing this, we shifted the pastor (pastors) to the role of recruiting, equipping, and encouraging all the ministers to do their acts of service.

We even began training a team of people to do the calling and shut-in ministry, because this was not my area of giftedness. This did not mean I never called on those who were in times of need. But we made a shift in our philosophy of ministry and leadership and began to follow the biblical vision of all God's people doing significant ministry. With time, we shifted to a gift-based approach and found leaders (the vast majority volunteers) to direct these ministries.

This is not a book on spiritual gifts and church structure, but I would recommend that every church seeking to make a U-Turn take time to study and use one of the many excellent tools that can help them adopt a biblical vision of leadership and spiritual gifts.[2] As Corinth began to see every person as having gifts to offer, and many people having leadership gifts rather than just the pastor, things really began to shift.

Roadblock #2: Antiquated Committee Structures

Pre-U-Turn Snapshot

One systemic roadblock to an effective U-Turn is the existence of rigid committee structures that continue year after year and decade after decade in many churches. When I came to Corinth Church, there was an extensive network of committees. In effect, these groups set the direction for each of the church ministries. The problem was that many of the people on these committees had no personal investment in the ministry they influenced.

For example, more than half of the youth committee members were *not* actually involved in the youth ministry on a week-to-week basis. They were *not* invested. They did *not* know what was happening in the ministry. They were *not* in relationship with the students.

But they had veto power over all that happened in the youth ministry.

This was not a healthy or effective leadership structure.

It made no sense.

It did not work.

But it was the structure the church had used for years. This was also true of the children's committee, the missions committee, and other areas of ministry in the church. There were people offering leadership, setting the budget, and giving direction to ministries in which they had no personal investment.

U-Turn Philosophy and Action

In a short time we made a shift from a committee model to what we called Ministry Teams. We dismantled all of the committees and removed those who were not committed to actually serve in that ministry. Then we gathered people with leadership gifts, a high level of involvement, and a sincere commitment to a specific area of ministry. These people provided leadership because they were aware of what was happening in the ministry through personal involvement. And they loved the people in the ministry.

Once we had active participants in a specific area of ministry taking leadership, the U-Turn was much easier. We no longer had people with no stake in a ministry, stamping *Veto* on exciting new ministry initiatives just because they did not like the idea or thought it was frivolous.

You might be thinking, *Didn't some of the people who were removed from the committee structure feel hurt or get upset?* You already know the answer! Of course they did. But we sought to be gentle. We tried to help connect them in new areas where they had a personal passion and stake in that ministry.

Most of the frustration blew over quite quickly. I wish I could say every step of a U-Turn is joyful and the road is always lined with tulips and daffodils, but I would be lying. Sometimes following Jesus and doing His will means sacrifice and struggle. But it is always worth it.

Roadblock #3: Faithless Finances

Pre-U-Turn Snapshot

Do you remember who held the purse strings and managed the money on the first church board in history? His name was Judas Iscariot, and his motives were not always as pure as the driven snow.[3]

I am not saying that most chairmen of deacon boards or finance teams are evil and should not be trusted. But I do want to point out a distinct finance-related leadership challenge that can get in the way of a healthy U-Turn movement. Sometimes the people who handle the church budget want to run the church like a business. They set budgets based on what we can afford, what we can manage, and what makes the most sense. Some even feel like their job is to protect the money from being used.

Early in my time at Corinth Church, we faced this dilemma. The need for ongoing U-Turn activity in the area of finances became profoundly apparent. In our church tradition, we have deacons who handle the finances. And every year some of the board members rotate off and new deacons come on. This means we had a new group of deacons on an annual basis that needed to learn that their job didn't exist to keep people from spending money. They had to be taught to lead by faith, trust in God, and invest in ministry, not block it.

Don't get me wrong. These were wonderful, godly people. They loved Jesus and His church. They cared deeply. But they also had a very specific financial background and disposition that led them to function with a level of frugality that hindered vision-based ministry.

They had to learn that they were not there to make sure the youth ministry didn't spend frivolously. They were not there to cut, slash, and veto money for ministry. They were called to be visionary, faith-filled leaders who sought God and people for the resources needed to do what God had called the church to do.

U-Turn Philosophy and Action

Although wisdom is needed and fiscal responsibility is important, the church is fundamentally different from a business. We walk by faith and not by sight. We trust God to provide what we don't have. If all we do is what we can manage and afford, then let's face it: We don't need God. We can do it ourselves.

One of the biggest shifts we made was that we began to talk about what God wanted to do in the church and not about what we could afford. My mantra was "If we are following the vision of God, He will provide all we need." Our board members and other leaders began to look at their roles differently. Their job was to pray, make wise decisions, be good stewards, and help direct the resources to God's vision and plan for the church. This was new for many people, but as God showed up and moved in mighty ways, enthusiasm grew.

One of our first budgets after beginning our U-Turn had close to a 40 percent increase from the previous year. It made no sense . . . from a human perspective. The church had not grown enough to sustain it. But as we looked at God's vision and where He was leading us, we were sure God would provide.

In one year we added a new building (the Ministry Training Center), added a new worship service, hired a new full-time pastor, and increased vision for ministry in six new areas.

We were out on a limb! We were up a creek! We were living on the edge! You get the idea.

Guess what happened? God showed up! He provided all we needed and more. Over the next few years, the funds came in as the vision grew. The resources came from a host of different sources. Regular attendees who always gave felt led to give more because they saw the vision. People who had never given much were inspired to participate in God's new work. New people came and they gave. Even people from outside of the church heard about what was happening and wanted to invest in eternity.

I wish I could say we had some tightly knit strategy and campaign, but we did not. We simply asked, "What does God want us to do?" Then we presented it to the congregation, prayed, and moved forward. I can still remember a year (early in the U-Turn process) when a key volunteer leader, Fred Burgess, stood at my side as we each presented the vision for the coming year. Fred was a patriarch in the church, a godly man, and a faithful volunteer. The board had adopted a budget that was more aggressive than I would have recommended . . . they were getting the vision. As Fred spoke with faith and confidence, I could feel the congregation being touched by God. They approved an aggressive and visionary budget. That year God did it again. He provided. And He got the glory because there was no way we could have done it on our own.

If a church begins with the question, "What can we afford?" they will never enter the realm of faith. They may meet their goals, but not walk in the adventure of following God to the places He wants to take them.

Once, after we were a few years into our U-Turn, things were getting tight. We had set a visionary budget and it looked like we might not have enough to do everything we had planned. The church board was getting nervous. They were about to pull the reins in and start cutting programs and staff. It seemed like the "responsible" and "sensible" thing to do.

Then someone in the board meeting said, "Before we start cutting and running, maybe we should take a week to fast and pray for God's provision. Let's give God a chance to surprise us." Everyone agreed to hold off cuts until we really took the time to seek God.

The following Sunday, a member of the deacon board came and found me after the last worship service. He escorted me into the office where they counted the offering. There on the table was a huge mound of cash and checks. Since I was never in the room when they counted, I asked, "Is that good?" The looks on the faces of the deacons answered my question. That Sunday, the church had the largest offering in more than a century. Somebody said, "I vote that we keep walking by faith!" Then we paused and prayed, thanking God for proving himself faithful . . . again.

Roadblock #4: Lack of Appreciation

Pre-U-Turn Snapshot

Those who lead and serve at a significant level should be blessed and acknowledged on a regular basis. Many congregations, prior to making a U-Turn, miss this important component and it keeps them from being an effective and dynamic church or ministry. Pastors, staff members, or other leaders can be taken for granted. Acknowledgement can be sparse. And criticism can actually be leveled at these faithful and hardworking leaders. Some congregations can be tough on their leaders and quick to point out what went wrong, what could be better, or how previous leaders "did it differently." In this kind of climate, U-Turn movement and momentum is hard to maintain.

U-Turn Philosophy in Action

In a U-Turn church, there should be a commitment to celebrate, rejoice, bless, and affirm those who serve faithfully. They can be staff members or volunteers. When something is worth encouraging, we need to lift it up and celebrate. This kind of attitude and climate of rejoicing is powerful and contagious.

Early on in my time at Corinth Reformed Church, I made a commitment to write two encouraging notes each day of the week. I did not announce this as a strategy (because it wasn't). I just knew that there were a lot of people leading and serving, and many of them needed a little encouragement.

It was amazing how people responded to these brief hand-written notes. I had leaders and faithful servants come to me and say things like, "I have been serving in this ministry for ten years, and that was the first personal thank-you note I have received." This was both affirming and heartbreaking. I think sometimes we assume someone else is blessing and affirming our leaders, when the truth is, many serve with little or no thanks. I even had one leader come to me after I had been doing this for some time, and he told me that he had kept the notes I sent him in a box on his dresser. He said, "When I get discouraged or wonder if God can use me, I take out your notes and reread them and remember that God can and does use me!"

Wow, what a reminder of the importance of blessing.

In a short time, other leaders caught on to the importance of blessing those who serve and they began to write notes on a regular basis. As a matter of fact, I was the recipient of many of those notes of blessing (an unplanned bonus for me!). In time, we actually had someone design a series of thank-you cards with the church logo, and we made these available to all the staff, board members, and key volunteer leaders. This was another way to reinforce the importance of offering encouragement to leaders.

My wife, Sherry, planned a yearly celebration for all the children's volunteers just to bless and thank them for their ministry. She put the cost into her budget and put on a wonderful party with gifts for all those who had served that year. They were not big or expensive gifts, but they were thoughtful and greatly appreciated.

Deb Rose, the choir director, held a yearly Christmas party at her home as well as another party in May to celebrate all the great things that had happened during the choral year. The express intention of these gatherings was to thank and bless those who had served so faithfully through the music ministry of the church. In addition, she would lavish these faithful servants with encouragement, cards, and thanks throughout the year. People felt so loved and affirmed that almost all of the choir members came back to serve again, year after year. They loved being part of this ministry, but they also felt appreciated.

This same spirit pervaded the other areas of ministry. A spirit of blessing poured over the church, and people knew they were valued, needed, and making a difference for Jesus. This spirit propelled us forward on our U-Turn adventure.

Roadblock #5: Slots Instead of Significance

Pre-U-Turn Snapshot

Churches that have not yet caught the U-Turn vision often use people to fill ministry slots. They simply look for a warm body or a person with a pulse and put them somewhere that needs a little help. This haphazard approach falls short on a number of levels. First, people's gifts are not used to their fullest capacity. Second, highly qualified leaders end up discouraged and even leave a church because they feel that they have much more to offer and actually want to invest at a higher level in the church. Third, this approach falls short because it lacks a comprehensive vision to get the right people in the right place for the right reasons. The idea that *everyone* is fitted for *every* ministry is inconsistent with the teaching of Scripture.[4]

Many wonderful books have been written, and curriculums have been developed, to help churches make a shift that will mobilize and connect people in ministry around their gifts.[5]

U-Turn Philosophy and Action

Over about three years, early in our U-Turn process, Corinth Church committed to do all we could to find gifted leaders and connect them in significant roles of ministry that fit their passions and unique wiring. We used the Networking resources developed by Willow Creek Church.[6] We also used organic connections to discover where people were passionate. Then we connected each person in places of ministry where they could thrive and feel the amazing gratification of the Holy Spirit of God working through them to touch the lives of others.

One very helpful and practical way we developed this philosophy was teaching about it in the new members' class. We even did a gifts survey that helped us identify the gifts, passions, and talents of new people in the church.

The issue is not the particular curriculum or tool you use. The key for a healthy U-Turn is that your church commits to helping people find a place of service and leadership that fits their unique gifting.

Roadblock #6: The Spiritual Maturity of Leaders

Pre-U-Turn Snapshot

In many churches, there is an unspoken assumption that the people in leadership positions are spiritually mature and committed to regular spiritual disciplines that lead to ongoing growth. It is rare to hear someone ask an elder or deacon, "Are you digging deep into God's Word and spending consistent time in prayer?" In the same way, we operate with an unspoken confidence that the women's ministry coordinator and the children's ministry volunteers are walking closely with God.

Through my years of ministry, I have learned that this is not a wise assumption.

The truth is, many of our church leaders, including pastors, staff members, board members, and key volunteers are simply not going as deep in their faith journey as they would want or we might think. If this is the case, and we don't help these leaders in their journey of spiritual maturity, it will be hard to make a U-Turn.

Churches that are hungry to see renewal and revival will begin with their leaders. When our key influencers in the church are falling deeper and deeper in love with God and spending time sitting at the feet of the Savior, they will make a personal U-Turn and the church will follow. When our leaders are overflowing with the Holy Spirit, they will be ready to take the steps and make the changes that are needed.

U-Turn Philosophy and Action

One of the key steps we took at Corinth Church in our U-Turn journey was a concerted effort to create a web of accountability for our church board members. We were clear that if a person was called by God to leadership, spiritual growth should and could be expected. With this in mind, we established a three-tiered process to help each board member go deeper.

Small Groups. First, we set up small groups among our board members. They would spend about thirty minutes of our monthly meeting in these groups. This would be a time to share what God was doing in their lives, talk about what they were learning from the Word of God, and they would also pray together. Surprisingly, this addition of significant spiritual interaction at our board meeting did not make it run longer; in fact, our meetings became shorter! It turned out that as our leaders committed themselves to ongoing spiritual growth (on a daily basis as well as in their small groups), there was less contention and arguing in our meetings. A sweet spirit of unity grew in our midst. Of course we would still debate and express varied perspectives, but there was a humility and unity that pervaded our meetings, they moved along smoothly with a growing sense of joy and purpose.

Accountability. Second, we took time for accountability in our monthly meetings. Each board member would keep a journal of their daily time in the Word and in prayer. Then when their small group met, they would tell each other how they did in the previous month. They were honest and vulnerable with each other. They helped each other grow in their commitment to personal spiritual growth.

As we moved a few months into this new season of leadership expectations, many of the elders and deacons came to me, one-on-one, and started thanking me for the challenge and accountability because, as they readily admitted, "I really did not spend much time growing my own spiritual life until I was challenged to! This has been great for me."

What we discovered as we pressed on was that the leadership culture impacts the whole church. As our board members began to grow in their walk with God, their families were impacted, their marriages were strengthened, and their example overflowed to the church.

This should not surprise us! Leaders lead. If our leaders are not passionate about their faith and walking close with Jesus, why should we expect our church members to be growing? We discovered this was so important to our board members that we began creating the same kind of accountability and opportunity for spiritual growth for the staff and other key volunteers in the church.

Another wonderful example of this commitment to help leaders grow came when my wife, Sherry, realized that most of her volunteers for the children's ministry midweek program were heavily engaged in serving, but that they also needed to receive and be encouraged in their faith. When this hit her, she implemented a new approach: They would come to serve at the Wednesday night program, but only minister two-thirds of the time. One-third of the time, Sherry would lead a devotional, teach them, and invest in their spiritual growth. Once this move was made, her volunteers increased and the turnover at the end of the year dropped significantly. Many of the leaders actually told Sherry and others, "I love working with the kids, but one of the highlights of my week is what I learn when I get input time for my spiritual life on Wednesdays."

Sherry prepared a devotional and teaching time based on the lesson they were bringing the children. Then she would give this same message and lead a time of prayer for three rotating groups of leaders through the evening. It was a great tool for investing in leaders, and they loved it. Again, we discovered that the leaders were hungry to grow and excited to receive encouragement in their spiritual journey.

Help and Direction. Third, we provided help and direction for spiritual growth in the lives of our leaders. We did not just tell them to read their Bibles and pray. We provided a reading guide to give direction in a walk through the Bible and taught new ways to pray. We gave our leaders practical tools to help them succeed.

You can probably guess the results. As our leaders grew in their spiritual lives, it impacted the whole spirit and direction of the congregation. This had a powerful impact on our U-Turn experience. In a sense, a number of personal and small U-Turns combined to become a tipping point for the congregation.

Often we begin by trying to change the whole congregation. A better strategy is to start with the leaders.

Presently, I am pastor of Shoreline Community Church, and you can already guess that the leadership team, staff members, and key volunteer leaders are being challenged in their personal spiritual growth. We actually provide a weekly Bible reading guide that follows the Sunday worship service themes and passages. In fact, the whole church is provided a weekly Bible reading guide.[7] We also give weekly prayer direction and we teach a new approach to prayer each month of the year. We even provide a weekly passage to commit to memory and some personal and group reflection questions. To cap it off, we always have one or two Christian books or resources that are recommended for personal study.

These resources are recommended for the whole church, but they are strongly encouraged for all of our church leaders. If they already have a personal reading plan and developed spiritual disciplines, we encourage them to keep doing that. But if they need some direction that is strategic and follows the flow of where the church is going, we make sure they have it.

Your church can do this. If you want to see the church make a God-honoring U-Turn, start by challenging and supporting your leaders (board members, staff, children's volunteers, youth leaders, any and all leaders) as they take the steps needed to grow in their faith journey.

Remember Susan, the woman who was considering moving on to another church? Well, she stayed, and I am so glad she did!

God has used her in a number of significant positions of leadership and influence. Her gifts and passions are being unleashed, and she is delighted to invest more of her life in the local church.

Bob's Reflections on Unleashing Leaders

In our tradition, in my Reformed and Protestant background, we communicated theologically and biblically that we believed, like Corinth Reformed Church, in "the priesthood of all believers."[8] That was our statement. But in reality, that wasn't usually the way we practiced.

In Faith Church's story, we discovered that unleashing leaders and living out the priesthood of all believers proved successful. When we incorporated it, God blessed it. Every member is a minister. As Kevin did, I joked around once in a while and said we should actually have ordination services for every member as a minister. Faith Church was not intentional at becoming a priesthood-of-all-believers functioning church; we just ended up that way. Reflecting back on it, we can now pass on the importance of living it out. We stumbled upon a key factor that if all churches intentionally sought to function as a priesthood-of-all-believers church, they would be that much more on track with making the U-turn.

How did we begin to function this way? First of all, I really do take seriously the priesthood of all believers, but never intentionally applied that principle before. Secondly, I realized that I can't do it all. And I shouldn't do it all. People are gifted in many areas of ministry that I am not. People are smarter, more equipped, and overall a better fit than I am in many areas. It is biblical for the gifts God gives others to function in them to their fullest.

At Faith Church, the pastor was expected to do all of the calling, all home visitation, and all hospital visitation. Now, when a baby is born, a woman from either the prayer team or the children's department will go to the hospital with a gift bag to welcome that little one into our church family and pray with them. We receive positive feedback when members of a person's small group show up at the hospital. They tell us how important that is because they shared so much together as a small group and now they got to share in the joy and be there for them. We also received positive feedback such as "Thank goodness it's not Pastor Bob coming when I'm looking like this!" The mentality that the pastor doesn't have to do it all has permeated our church. The priesthood of all believers makes complete sense, and you can think of every single area of ministry, including preaching, where God can use the various members of the body of Christ to work together as a unit.

If I find a person who has the humility, the passion, spiritual gifts, and talent for an area of ministry, there is nothing I would rather do than unleash that person and trust him or her to do that ministry in the church. Faith Church is a place of healing for people whose marriages are broken. The priesthood of all believers was modeled, from the team that was formed to study it, to the people who donated ten acres of land with a beautifully designed home that would perfectly fit this purpose, to the woman that was unleashed to lead this ministry. The marriage hospital, called The Ravines, is up and running, where couples both locally and far away come to work on their marriages. It was originally designed as a last-resort resort (and it really has a resort-like setting), but has recently included a good-to-great element where couples that already have a good marriage can come together on a retreat to improve their marriages.

And all of this takes place by unleashing leaders. Look right in front of you at the rich resources God has placed in your church. Release those resources and enjoy seeing God network His people.

U-Turn Exercises and Activities

U-Turn Exercise—Time to Encourage

Take a first step in growing a culture of blessing. Make a list of three to five leaders who are faithfully serving your church. Take time to write them a note, give them a call, send them an e-mail, give them a tweet, or even get them a little gift. Let this be the start of a new discipline in your life and something you encourage other people in your church to do.

U-Turn Exercise—Time to Train

Identify one group of leaders that you influence. Make space for some kind of training or equipping on a weekly or monthly basis. Be sure to include some kind of accountability, where leaders are able to share what God is teaching them in their personal time with Him, and where they report how they are doing in developing personal spiritual disciplines.

U-Turn Reflection Questions

Gather with some leaders and key influencers from your church, read this chapter (either ahead of time or together), and talk about the following questions:

- Does our church have a healthy understanding of all believers as ministers in the church and not only professional clergy? What can we do to grow a more biblical vision of who is called to minister?
- Do our committee structures help or hinder effective U-Turn activity? What adjustments might we make to strengthen our leadership culture?
- How would you describe the way our leadership views finances? Is our first question, "What can we afford?" or "What does God want

to do?" How can we become more faithful in our understanding and use of our finances?

- What can we do to train and equip our leaders more effectively?

U-Turn Prayers

Gather with church friends, leaders, or small-group members and pray in the following directions:

- Pray that every person who is part of your church will see themselves as ministers and will find their place of service.
- Ask God to deepen the faith of your leaders (in particular those who handle the church finances) so that there will be a visionary trust that God will provide. Pray that your church will do things that only God could accomplish so that He will get the glory.
- Pray for the spiritual maturity of your leaders. Ask God to take them to places of depth and growth they have never experienced before.

7

High Expectations

by Kevin G. Harney

Everyone wants to be part of something big and world-changing. . . .
This rarely happens when we have low expectations.

I received a call from a pastor who was in the middle of a doctoral program on church growth and health. He asked if I would meet with him and talk about the ministry of Corinth Church. We were about eight years into our U-Turn process, and the church had doubled in size, doubled again, and was continuing on a healthy growth trajectory.

This pastor explained that he was examining eight distinct kinds of churches, and he saw Corinth as a "high expectation church." I was not sure what this meant, but I agreed to meet with him.

After a couple of hours of conversation, he had the information he needed for his study. He explained that Corinth really did call people to higher levels of commitment, spiritual growth, fellowship, giving, and service than most of the churches he had studied in his doctoral program. He found it interesting that people were drawn to a church that set the bar so high.

I explained that I did not see Corinth as a "high expectation church" as much as a "biblical expectations church." It was Jesus who said, *"If anyone would come after me, he must deny himself and take up his cross daily and follow me."* [1] The call of the Savior is the commitment of our whole life to Him. When Jesus calls a man or woman to himself, He invites us to lay down our lives and surrender everything.

The U-Turn at Corinth Church was propelled forward because we called people to radical transformation, sacrificial giving, passionate worship, and growing surrender to the One who gave His life for us on the cross.

High expectations did not drive people away; they drew people in.

As a matter of fact, a whole generation of young adults was attracted to the church when we added an in-depth Bible teaching time on Sunday evenings, where we went through the Bible chapter-by-chapter for three years. A whole group of twenty-somethings began coming because they were hungry for more than what they had been getting. They all sat in the front of the worship space every week as we dug into the Word. This group became a catalyst for a young adult ministry and leaders for the future of the church. A number of them have moved into full-time Christian service.

We did not set out to have high expectations. But we knew that if we were going to have a sustained and God-honoring U-Turn, it would mean calling people to radical discipleship. Doing church as usual, shooting for the lowest common denominator, and keeping the sheep well fed and in the pen simply was not going to be enough.

Expecting Intimacy With God

A U-Turn church is not about attracting more people, filling seats, or stemming the tide of decline. At the heart of it all is the desire to see people grow intimate with the God who made them, loves them, and saved them. When Jesus was asked what matters most in the entire universe, the first thing He said was, *"Love the Lord your God with all your heart and with all your soul and with all your mind."* [2] Nothing matters more than this.

Corinth Church always had a passion to see people grow in their love for Jesus. In the U-Turn process, this commitment became more focused, and we worked at finding ways to help people grow deeper in their relationship with the Savior. In the last chapter, we looked at how we raised expectations for leaders and helped keep them accountable for personal spiritual growth. As we moved forward on our U-Turn journey, these same expectations became part of the fabric of the church life. From adults to students, part of our U-Turn was helping people become dissatisfied with just showing up for church, punching the spiritual clock, and going home.

We worked with each ministry in the church to help people develop spiritual maturity and engage in personal spiritual disciplines. Children were encouraged to know and meditate on Scripture. Teens were engaging in serving by using their spiritual gifts. Adults were challenged to pray with passion and listen for the still, small voice of the Spirit. Children began learning to talk to Jesus like a friend. Students were being held accountable to have regular quiet times when they could sit at the Savior's feet. Adults were reminded that daily engagement with the truths of the Bible is normal fare for a follower of Jesus.

The message from the pulpit, in classes, small groups, and in every part of the church ministry was that spiritual growth is a natural and normal part of our faith. It is not enough to draw from the well once or twice a week when we gather for a corporate time of worship. Instead, we can each drink deeply of the living water of God's presence as we walk through our own daily journey of faith. Following Jesus is about a radical commitment of all we are so that we grow as His disciples.

Some years ago, I had a chance to sit with a woman in my family and share the simple message of the gospel. She had heard it many times before, but this time her heart was more open and tender. When I asked her if she was ready to accept Jesus and cross the line of faith, she said, "I think so, but I'm scared!"

Over the next half hour she shared three distinct areas of fear. Her final one was this: "I am afraid of what God might call me to do." She was totally honest. She had watched a number of our family members become Christians, and each one went through a radical transformation. Their lives were changed forever. She admitted her fear that God might call her to significant change.

My response surprised her . . . and me.

I said, "You *should* be afraid of that!" We went on to discuss the reality that following Jesus means surrendering everything. It means laying down all we have and are on the altar of grace because our Savior gave everything to redeem us. After a very frank discussion, she said she was ready to receive Jesus.

In another encounter, a man who had been visiting the church told me he was almost ready to receive Jesus, but he did not want to jump in lightly. His words were something like "This is the biggest decision of my life! This is bigger than when I got married. This is bigger than when I had kids. This is huge!"

I assured him that he was right. I was impressed that he saw the gravity of the moment. He actually decided not to take the leap that night, but a week later when we met again, he was ready. He received Jesus with a profound awareness that he was committing to a life-changing relationship, not simply a routine of attending weekly worship services.

A U-Turn church sets high expectations for personal spiritual engagement and growth. There is no other way. This is the call of Jesus and we can invite people to no less.

In recent years, there has been a wonderful focus on developing a number of new programs and resources that help us move people forward on a trajectory of spiritual growth that fits them. There are amazing books and even emerging online resources that can be used in the lives of believers and the local church. As your church seeks to raise the bar in the area of personal spiritual growth, take time to study some of the resources introduced in the endnotes of this book.[3]

Expecting Involvement Through Joyful Service

Once people begin to grow in their personal walk with the Savior, serving is a natural by-product. When we love Jesus, we grow to love His children. A U-Turn church will call people to connect in the body of Christ on many levels. One of the most important is in the area of serving.

There are Pew-Sitters and Heavy Hitters in the kingdom of God. A U-Turn church calls people to a level of involvement that stretches them and calls them to take up the basin and towel and wash feet just as Jesus has called us to do.[4]

For a season in the life of many churches, it was popular to set the bar very low, offer people a lot, and free people to hang back and do very little. I remember getting flyers in the mail for a few new church plants in our community right in the middle of our U-Turn process. I took a moment and prayed for God's blessing on those new works. But honestly, I was a bit skeptical. As I read their invitation flyers, they all had a very similar theme and tone. I would summarize it like this: *"If you are tired of churches that ask for too much and don't entertain you, come try our church! We will give you what you want and meet your needs."* Of course they said it in more clever ways, but that was the message. Now, many years later, those churches are either closed or struggling. I think the reason is that they were not honest. They promised much and asked little. This is not the U-Turn philosophy.

There will be people who come to your church and need time to connect and find their place, but this should not be a long-term process. There will be people who come with broken hearts or with ministry fatigue from serving at another church. Give them appropriate time to be refreshed. But we must always remember that involvement in the life of the church builds relational bridges, grows people, and gives purpose and meaning. Serving God, His people, and the community around your church should be a normal part of every believer's faith journey.

At Corinth, we began to use a couple of great resources to help existing members and new attendees discover their gifts and begin serving.[5] We went so far as to include a gifts survey in the new members' class and let people know that serving in the church and the community are normal practices for believers. We took the results of their survey and put it in our database so we could strategically invite these people to service opportunities that fit their gifting and passions. We discovered that the people who found a place to serve also made friends, experienced purpose, and became an active part of the church community.

Along with the call to serve, a U-Turn church will teach people that serving is not enough. We need to do it with the *right attitude*. In congregations that are grinding through a status quo approach to church life, there can be people who work very hard in the church, but their attitude can be poor.

They say things like, "I do this ministry because no one else will!" They complain about how much they do compared to everyone else. They grumble and whine while they serve Jesus and His church.

In your U-Turn journey, call people to serve faithfully but also joyfully. Remind them that it is an amazing privilege to serve the King of Kings and care for His beloved bride, the church.

Linda came up to me and began droning on about how hard she worked at her ministries. She complained about how many people did nothing, and how she stepped up so often to cover for them. She was volunteering in two specific areas of church ministry and was at the church ten to fifteen hours a week.

She did a lot, she really did.

And she did it well!

But she seemed unhappy and negative most of the time.

Have you ever run into this? She was a faithful worker, she did her ministry with excellence, but her attitude stunk!

I finally sat down for a meeting with Linda. I tried to be gentle. I listened to all her complaints. Then I said, "Linda, we are so thankful for your service, but you seem unhappy. If you want to step out of these two areas of ministry, we will find other volunteers to lead them."

She seemed shocked!

She said, "I love my ministry. I don't want to stop."

I pointed out that if she loved her ministry so much, she would not complain all the time. This became a moment of reckoning. She honestly had no idea how much she whined and griped. She was not aware that most people thought she did not enjoy her ministry.

After this conversation she changed her whole tone. She became joyful! She really did. Linda just needed someone to hold up a mirror and help her see how her disposition looked. She needed someone to explain to her how her attitude was impacting others. Once she realized the message she was sending, she adjusted her attitude and kept serving faithfully and joyfully.

In a U-Turn church we expect each person to serve. We also call people to express joy and delight at the privilege of serving God, His people, and a lost world. This does not mean it is always fun. It also does not mean we fake it and act like we are having a great time when we are not. What it does mean is that we seek to have the heart and attitude of Jesus. This means that joy comes through as the dominant attitude while we are serving.

Expecting Organic Outreach

Every believer is called to be God's salt and light in this world.[6] We are all expected to be ready to articulate our faith and the hope we have in Jesus.[7] Not every follower of Christ has the gift of evangelism, but we can all be witnesses to what He has done in our life and we can tell others who Jesus is. I call this organic outreach.[8] It is the process of letting the love of God, the message of Jesus, and the work of the Spirit flow through us in our everyday life.

Many Christians shy away from personal evangelism. They get nervous and make excuses as to why they should *not* do outreach. In a U-Turn church, every believer begins to feel the call to share their faith and gets a vision that they can do it, with the help of God.

At Corinth, we began training the congregation in personal outreach. We did the normal things like offering classes and equipping opportunities. We had a handful of enthusiastic people show up. In most cases, these were the people that already were committed to personal outreach and the ones who least needed the training.

Then something became profoundly clear. If we really expected everyone in the church to engage in outreach in their workplace, school, family, neighborhood, and our community, we would have to train *all of them*. The only place this could be done was during the weekend services. That's right! We committed to do an outreach series every year and use a part of this time to train every person in the church. If they would not come to our training, we would bring it to them.[9]

Instead of scaring people away and offending them, the congregation loved it. People felt empowered and equipped to do something they had always wanted to do but had never really engaged in. We saw immediate fruit come from this. All of a sudden we had hundreds of people feeling bold about loving, serving, and sharing in new ways.

We even structured the church around outreach and made sure that every ministry in the church was committed to doing outreach. Most of the leaders, both staff and volunteers, were excited about this new focus. Some were resistant at first, but with time everyone caught the vision. Our mantra was, "Everything is outreach!" If someone looked at their area of ministry and did not see the evangelistic potential, we would talk and pray until God showed us where the outreach connections were hiding and they always showed up.

Out of this journey I wrote a book called *Organic Outreach for Ordinary People* and then another one called *Organic Outreach for Churches*. These two books chronicle the journey of a personal conversion to evangelism and also how a whole church can reorient their ministry around the Great Commission. U-Turn churches have a commitment to share the love and message of Jesus and it becomes part of every aspect of their ministry.[10]

Expecting Generous Giving

Most churches face challenges when it comes to giving. Some pastors shy away from preaching and teaching on the biblical call to tithe and give offerings above the 10 percent. Others hit this topic hard when the giving dips, but avoid it if the offerings are strong. In a U-Turn church, there is an awareness that the work being done and the lives being touched are so important that everyone needs to give with sacrificial generosity as a normal part of their spiritual devotion.

This spirit must begin with the leaders. Pastors, staff members, board members, and other key influencers need to set the pace for this. There is a connection between a generous heart and faithful giving. If our leaders and key influencers are in love with God, passionate about the work of the church, and have a heart for the community, they will grow as givers. At Corinth Church, and now at Shoreline Community Church, I have always called the leaders to deep levels of commitment in the area of giving. If leaders don't feel this call, the church never will.

Once the leaders are on board, the message of generous giving needs to be communicated to the congregation and even to those who are new to the church. I am always quick to say that I don't get a bonus for new members or increased offerings. I do not work on a commission. My motivation for teaching about giving is the health, joy, and blessing that comes to the giver.

Some years ago, I wrote a book called *Seismic Shifts* and devoted three chapters to the topic of giving. This book focuses on some of the most important areas of the life of faith. Some might wonder why I would spend three chapters on this topic. The answer is, *"Where your treasure is, there your heart will be also."* [11]

There is a classic story about Rev. Peter Marshall when he was chaplain to the U.S. Senate. A man approached him and shared a personal struggle he was facing. It seems this man had always tithed, giving 10 percent toward God's work. When he had a modest income, this was easy. As a young man he made $20,000 a year and freely gave $2,000 to God's work. But over time his income continued to grow and grow. Now his annual income was $500,000 a year. He explained that there was no way he could afford to give a tithe of $50,000 a year to the church. It was just too much!

As the story goes, Rev. Marshall simply asked if they could pray. The respected pastor began to pray for this struggling man and asked God to help him learn to tithe again, even if it meant bringing his income all the way back down to $20,000 a year. Right in the middle of the prayer, the wealthy man stopped Marshall. He knew he was a mighty man of prayer and feared that God might actually take him seriously and reduce his income. "No, Dr. Marshall, that's not what I meant!" The point was made, and the man suddenly realized he could afford to tithe.

In a U-Turn church, people begin to give in new ways because they see the vision and their hearts beat with the heart of God. We raise the expectations in the area of giving because God has high expectations.

Just imagine a church where every person gave a tithe and even found joy in giving beyond the first 10 percent. The amount of ministry that could be done, missions that could be supported, and help for the local community would be staggering. When the U-Turn vision grows and ignites, giving follows. Resources flow to vision, and when God's vision is alive, people want to give.

Expecting Excellence

Excellence and perfection are two different things. No church will ever reach perfection, but a U-Turn church raises the bar and calls people to excellence for the sake of God. This is one of the shifts that moves through a church making a U-Turn. Contentment with mediocrity or poor ministry begins to erode and people want more.

Back in the days of Malachi, the people had forgotten that the God they worshiped was holy, worthy, and mighty beyond description. They were walking out to their sheep pen and finding the most mangy, sickly, worthless animal and bringing it to God as their act of worship. They were saying, "Here you go, God, this is my best . . . it is for you." Malachi asks the people, "How would your political leaders respond if you brought that kind of a gift to them?" The answer was clear. They would see right through the gift into their hearts and would not be pleased![12]

God was not interested in their scraps and garbage. He wanted their best offering, their finest effort, and their wholehearted devotion. This is what God wants from His people today.

Our worship songs should be the best we can offer, and our choral numbers should be an excellent offering. Our buildings should be cared for and not run-down. Our nursery care should be so good that when a visitor comes they are amazed by the space, care, and safety. Our children's programs should be well-planned, well-staffed, and a blessing to all the kids. Our missions and local outreach should be done in the absolute best possible way we can offer. No more wandering out to the sheep pen and grabbing the sickest lamb in our flock and offering it to God. It is time to seek excellence in all things.

To be sure, what is excellent will vary from church to church and God understands that. A church of five hundred in a college town with lots of music majors will have a different worship team than a congregation of seventy-five and no trained musicians. But both can give an excellent offering to God. Excellence is not about a level of performance, but a commitment to give God our best: our best music, teaching, service, nursery care, and everything else we do.

Expecting Change

One more expectation we must keep high as we travel the U-Turn road is an expectation of change. This is part of the landscape of a U-Turn church. There will always be change.

About six years into the U-Turn at Corinth Church, some of the leaders and church members were dealing with a bit of what I call "change fatigue." There had been many new challenges and changes through the years. During the annual congregational meeting, we were introducing yet another new ministry to reach out to our community with the love and message of Jesus. It would mean more money, time, and energy. It would mean more change.

I can still see one of the key leaders in the church standing up to speak his mind. He wanted everyone to know that he was ready to support this new initiative and he did think it was a good idea. Then he said something that made me laugh on the inside.

He said, "I will vote for this, and I will support it. But I want you to assure us that this will be the last change we make."

I refrained myself from chuckling and kept from saying what first came to my mind.

I said a quick, silent prayer.

I took a deep breath.

Then I said, "The only thing I can promise you is that if we keep following Jesus, growing His people, and reaching out with His love, we will always be changing." I was clear that our doctrine and commitment to God's Word would never change, but the way we did things would always be flexible. Change would continue to be part of our landscape if we were to remain a U-Turn church.

We live in a time in history when expectations seem to be lowered on a weekly basis. This is not the heartbeat of a U-Turn church. Jesus called us to surrender all to Him, to take up our cross, deny ourselves, and follow Him. His expectations are so high that the only way we can accomplish them is to cry out for the presence and power of the Holy Spirit to help us move forward. High expectations are not about a bunch of human goals we impose on the church. They are about seeking the will and heart of God in all things. As we do this, the expectations will be high, and the results will be glorious for the name of Jesus.

Bob's Reflections on High Expectations

Christians and churches ought to live with higher expectations than they do. A significant change in a U-Turn happens when the church expects more out of its leaders, its pastors, its elders, its deacons, and members.

Many years ago, I was at a conference at Saddleback Church. Rick Warren taught us that his church raised the bar of expectation, and every time they did, the people met the expectation. I had an epiphany of what could be. I was convicted that I was not leading a high expectation church, and I committed to raising the bar from that point on, for myself, for all of our leaders, and all of our members. Like Saddleback Church, when we expected more, people rose up to meet the expectation.

For example, when our church was being built, we had an opportunity to build a small room near the auditorium where people could purchase messages on cassette and CD, Bibles, books, and other material to encourage their spiritual growth. I recognized the need for someone with a creative mind and organizational skills to lead this ministry. Knowing my wife to have those gifts, I asked her if she would bring the dream of a bookstore into reality. At the initial sign-up, other gifted people volunteered to help develop this new ministry from scratch. Together, a vision was cast, the mission made clear, and the responsibilities divided. Soon the level of expected commitment grew along with the impact of the ministry church-wide. The volunteers were conscious that their role in the ministry was vital to its success in aiding the spiritual growth of others. When the expectations were outlined and the needs were made clear, volunteers stepped up to the plate and even helped recruit others to join in the ministry. They were blessed and appreciated for their responsiveness to the expectations that were set. This level of volunteer commitment has been phenomenal from the start, and continues at a very high level to this day.

I raised the bar of expectation in all areas. I encouraged and held our elders, deacons, and staff accountable in terms of their own commitment to serve the Lord. I asked each staff member, elder, and deacon these questions: "Where are you serving or volunteering? Are you tithing?" I try to model these things myself, and serve each summer in the nursery with my family.

We have a new members' class that people interested in becoming a member of Faith Church must take. We teach the vision of the church, our theology, and what is expected of them. We tell our potential members that if you are a follower of Jesus Christ, have professed that and become a member of Faith Church, you are expected to worship, to find a mini-church (small group), to tithe, and to serve.

We have many remarkable teams in place. Our Technical Arts Group (TAG) requires a high expectation for all the volunteers every week to control the light, sound, PowerPoint, and other technology. Our Worship Team has a high expectation for all the instrumentalists and vocalists. If they are not at Monday night practice, they cannot play on the weekend. Our Treasureland (children's ministry) Team members are expected to serve multiple services for their given week. Some members serve every week. Many other teams, not mentioned, also put in an incredible amount of hours. I am amazed by the humility and the accountability of these teams.

I believe raising the bar of expectation is a necessity for a church that is U-Turn-driven. People are honored when they are entrusted with high responsibility. They take ownership in their ministry. It keeps the momentum going. I thank the Lord for Rick Warren, for his encouragement and for his teaching me to expect more and watch God's people rise to the occasion. We are passing onto you the importance of high expectations. Enjoy the fruit that will follow.

U-Turn Exercises and Activities

U-Turn Exercise—Leadership Discussion

Have a discussion with your primary church leaders and influencers about the topic of high expectations. Invite each person to fill out the survey below and use this as a discussion starter:

How would you rate our church in each of the areas below on a scale from 1 to 10? (1 meaning we have low expectations and 10 meaning we have very high expectations).

1. Expecting people to have an intimate and growing relationship with God

   Low commitment expected   Normal expectations High expectations

   I————————————————————————————————I

   1   2   3   4   5   6   7   8   9   10

2. Expecting people to serve with a joyful heart

   Low commitment expected   Normal expectations High expectations

   I————————————————————————————————I

   1   2   3   4   5   6   7   8   9   10

3. Expecting people to reach out and share their faith in natural ways

   Low commitment expected   Normal expectations High expectations

   I————————————————————————————————I

   1   2   3   4   5   6   7   8   9   10

4. Expecting people to give generously

   Low commitment expected   Normal expectations High expectations

   I————————————————————————————————I

   1   2   3   4   5   6   7   8   9   10

5. Expecting people to do whatever they do in the church with a commitment to excellence

Low commitment expected   Normal expectations High expectations

I————————————————————————————————I

   1   2   3   4   5   6   7   8   9   10

6. Expecting change as a normal part of our church life

Low commitment expected   Normal expectations High expectations

I————————————————————————————————I

   1   2   3   4   5   6   7   8   9   10

Take one topic at a time and invite each person to share the score they gave your church. Let them say why they gave the score they did. After everyone has given their score for a specific area, ask for ideas on how the church could increase expectations in this part of your church life.

U-Turn Prayers

Gather with church friends, leaders, or small-group members and pray in the following directions:

- Pray for all those who are part of your church to hunger and long for a more intimate and dynamic relationship with Jesus.
- Ask God to stir up hearts so that more and more people will discover the joy of serving and using their gifts for God's glory.
- Thank God for the people who give with a generous heart, and pray for God to stir the hearts of those who have not yet discovered the blessing of giving.

8

Tough Skin and Soft Hearts

by Kevin G. Harney

*To press forward in the U-Turn process will demand a tender heart
and skin like a rhinoceros.
It is easy to have one or the other. It is quite difficult to have both!*

In every church I have served in the past three decades, I have felt the painful sting and heartache of being attacked by God's people. In my first church, a kind and helpful man sought me out early on in my ministry and offered his wisdom and insight on how the church should be led. When the senior pastor retired and I stepped in as the interim leader of the church, this gentleman came right into my office and began talking about how "the two of us" would set a new direction for the church. I was young, but I knew something was not right in this scenario. Red flags started popping up in my mind!

I explained to him that we had a board of elders and deacons, and they were the team of leaders who had been called and ordained to give direction to the church. I gently clarified that he and I would not be setting the direction for the future of the church, but the church board, with my leadership, would be taking care of the church vision.

He spun on me like a rabid dog!

I had never seen a person switch from kind and caring to angry and attacking so fast. He went on to wage a personal campaign to get me thrown out of the church. He went so far as to write a five-page, hand-written letter of attack. It was some of the meanest, twisted, and most dishonest propaganda I have ever read. When I got to the third page, he moved from attacking me and started in on my wife!

That was it! I was about to take off the gloves and go after the guy. Remember, I was young.

Thankfully, God gave me wisdom and I remembered a simple lesson I had learned from a pastor who had done some training with a bunch of us seminary students. Rev. Harold Korver, pastor of Emmanuel Reformed Church, taught us this powerful lesson:

> In the church you will find the healthiest and the sickest of humanity.
> This is how it has always been,
> this is how it will always be,
> this is how it should be . . .
> we are the church!

Those words resonated through my soul as I pondered how to respond to the attack campaign being waged against me. I could become hardhearted. Shut off my emotions. Do my best not to feel or care. I could let this mean-spirited and dishonest attack poison my soul. Or I could find the balance of having a tender heart, but thick skin. This was the start of my journey toward learning this important balance.

I ended up taking the attack letter to the church board and asking them to prayerfully deal with it. I knew that if I confronted this man, it would not end well. The board was amazing. They addressed it, put this man under formal church discipline, and much of the conflict settled . . . for a time. When the new pastor finally came, this same man tried to cozy up to him just like he had with me. Thankfully, the new church leader refused to let this man manipulate him. Sadly, this man started another attack against the new pastor, but this time he was a bit subtler.

Years later, in my second church, one of the first people to warmly greet me when I came as a candidate was the first to really come after me once I was a pastor on the church staff. He disagreed with me on a specific issue and pulled me aside after a board meeting. He let me know that if I opposed his opinion on this in a public setting he would "fight me and beat me."

The level of intensity and anger this man expressed was way out of proportion. He was coming after me because I was the new guy and I was young.

Once again, I recalled the words of Pastor Korver:

In the church you will find the healthiest and the sickest of humanity.
This is how it has always been,
this is how it will always be,
this is how it should be . . .
we are the church!

I decided not to fight or retaliate. This was tough for me because by nature, I am a fighter. But I weighed out the options, prayed for wisdom, and felt a public confrontation would not be in the best interests of the church. In the process, I tried to guard my heart from becoming hard. I tried to remain tender inside, but let my skin toughen up so that I would not get crushed and discouraged in my ministry.

In my third church, where I served for many years, one attack came from a strange source. A family that had lots of challenges and struggles had sought me out to give some support and counsel to their children. I was new in the church, and the congregation was still fairly small. I spent time trying to encourage their family members. I tried to support this husband and wife as they struggled in their marriage. They came to me for prayer and perspective at least a couple times a month for a number of years.

So when this couple asked to come and speak to the board about a number of concerns they had about me, I was a bit surprised. There was not another family in the church that I had invested more time, care, and pastoral energy into over those years.

I prepared the board before the couple came and asked that we simply listen, gather concerns, and pray for this family. I was at the meeting, but told the board that I would not argue or defend myself, but simply listen along with the board members.

When the couple entered, we prayed and then invited them to share whatever was on their hearts. They took out a list with about a dozen "concerns" about me and the church. One by one they walked through their list: "We have not been cared for enough." "Our children have not been supported by the pastor." "The worship services are not inspiring." Then they hit below the belt: "The preaching is not biblical." I sensed this last one was meant to cut deeply. On and on they went, for just under an hour.

When they were finished dismantling the church and the pastor (me), we asked if there was anything else they wanted to say. They said no. So we prayed and excused them.

After they left, we walked through each of their concerns and complaints and asked the questions: "Is there truth in what they have said?" "What can we learn from them?" and "What might we do differently in the future?"

To be honest, there were a few things they said that helped us shape some church direction for the future. But the board agreed that most of what they said was not true or helpful. Much of it was coming from their own pain and brokenness. The board members assured me that the comments about worship and my preaching were completely off-base and obviously mean-spirited.

As I went home that night, I faced yet another moment when I had to make some decisions. If I chose to replay the mental tapes of their words and attacks, it would crush my spirit and break my heart. But I did not want to become hardhearted. This was another time when I had to develop a thick skin so that I would not become bitter and angry. I needed to be sure my heart was still tender.

Like a refrain in a song, the words came back to me again:

In the church you will find the healthiest and the sickest of humanity.
This is how it has always been,
this is how it will always be,
this is how it should be . . .
we are the church!

Through the years, as I have tried to lead U-Turn movements in a handful of churches, I have learned that having thin skin will lead to bitterness and constant pain. Tough things happen in the church, and even more often in a U-Turn church. Thick skin is a must for pastors, board members, and any leader in a church that is going to seek to move in new directions for the glory of God. We must also keep our hearts tender. We cannot become cynical and apathetic. If we do, it will be impossible to press on with the U-Turn vision.

As you read this book and consider leading a U-Turn movement in your church, I can assure you that there will be moments when loving and kind people will turn mean, and you will have ample opportunity to toughen your skin and keep your heart tender.

Well-Intentioned Dragons

Years ago, early in my ministry, I picked up a book called, *Well-Intentioned Dragons* by Marshall Shelley.[1] To this day, it is one of my favorite books on leadership. It helps leaders learn how to deal with conflict and problem people in the church. Shelley's basic premise is that many of the people in the church who battle, fight, and seek to undermine a new and healthy direction for a church actually think they are doing the right thing. They are "well-intentioned."

This was very helpful for me as I led during the U-Turn process. Instead of becoming angry with people or hoping they would leave, I tried to understand why they were fighting and resisting. In many cases I learned that they were trying to do the right thing. It was their way of loving the church. Knowing this kept my heart tender toward them.

This did not mean I agreed with them. It did not mean I let them poison the well with a bitter attitude or undermine where God was taking the church. But it helped me listen, minister, and care for them, even when we disagreed.

Instead of seeing those who dissented as enemies and bad people, I did my best to see them as brothers and sisters who loved the church and Jesus. They simply were not able to get the big picture of what God was doing. By looking at them as "well-intentioned dragons," I was able to minister to them instead of attacking and retaliating.

This led to some amazing things. First of all, in our U-Turn at Corinth, I know of only two families that left the church. One family was concerned we were getting "too big." Another did not like the "new music." I actually helped these two families find new churches and did what I could to pastor them as they moved on.

There was no mass exodus of unhappy church members. There was not a group that left all together and started a new church down the street. Virtually everyone who was at the church when I came and when we began the U-Turn process was there ten years later. I am convinced that a lot of this was due to the fact that God kept my heart soft and caring, but my skin tough enough not to become devastated when people would fight and push back against the new church direction.

Another wonderful result was that many of the strongest resisters and most fiery dragons became our greatest supporters. There was one woman who stood in the way of two distinct areas of ministry we were seeking to develop in our U-Turn. She had a high level of leadership and ownership in these areas and did not want to let go. She was resistant in a passive-aggressive way. But as we talked, she began to get the vision. The leadership challenged her to try getting on board, and she came around about a year later. With time, we became great friends and partners in ministry. Once she was a supporter of the new church direction, she helped bring others along with her.

A third surprise was that many people had no idea they were being cantankerous. They were trying to protect their church, preserve their traditions, and stand up for Jesus. They saw themselves as guardians of the truth and the future of the church. As we were able to gently hold up a mirror so they could see how they were acting, most of them were surprised at what they saw.

In time, they embraced the new direction and were able to see that we were not compromising on beliefs or doctrine. As a matter of fact, they began to see that the church was deepening its commitment to missions and intensifying its dedication to bringing the love and gospel of Jesus to our community.

Thick, But Not Too Thick!

I wish I could give a formula or simple steps to making it through a U-Turn without getting crushed or becoming hardhearted. It is not that simple. But I can give my best ideas to help you along the way. Here are my suggestions for helping you keep a tender heart and grow thick skin so you can move forward on the journey.

1. Keep your eyes on Jesus.

The writer of Hebrews invites us to *"Fix our eyes on Jesus . . ."*[2] When times are tough and we feel under attack, we can remember that Jesus endured the cross for us. He knew that His suffering would bring a harvest of souls into the kingdom of God.

When verbal bullets fly, when stares feel like daggers, and when dear friends act mean-spirited, look to Jesus. Fix your eyes on Him. Remember what He suffered for your sake. Then press on. It will be worth it.

In the moments when you feel like giving up on the vision God has planted in the heart of your church, remember Jesus as He carried the cross up to Calvary. Thank Him for pressing on for you. Then commit to press on for His sake.

2. Keep inviting people into the adventure.

Invite people into the excitement of the U-Turn process, then invite them again, and when you think it makes no sense at all, invite them one more time. There are early adopters, late adopters, and everything in-between. Don't assume that just because someone has resisted for the first year that they will never get on board. As I shared earlier, some of the greatest advocates and most faithful workers for this new vision will be people who resisted at first. Make a point of creating on-ramps for the vision as often as possible.

3. Learn the value of apathy.

In most cases, apathy is a bad thing. But when you are committed to a U-Turn in your church, one way to guard your heart is to learn the value of apathy. There are some things you should not care about. If you need everyone to be happy, on the same page, and equally excited about the new church direction, you won't make it far down the U-Turn road. If you can learn not to care if a few people are grumbling or a long-term friend just doesn't get why the church is so focused on people who are not part of the church, you will be much healthier.

Don't get me wrong. I am not saying you should not care at all. But if you care excessively, you will never move forward. There will be times you will need to say, deep in your heart, "Because I am committed to the vision God has given our church, I can't get pulled into the frustration and concerns of every person who is resisting the U-Turn." In short, there will be times you will need to employ selective and strategic apathy.

4. Never encourage snipers.

In many churches there is an unhealthy practice of letting one person step up and speak on behalf of many others. There will be people who want to come to the church board or into a staff meeting and say something like, "I have talked with many people in the church and they all feel that the new music is not honoring to God. It is not reverent enough." Or "I have had dozens of people seek me out and tell me that they do not like the new direction the church is going." Or "Quite a few people have told me that they will stop giving their offerings to the church if we don't . . ."

I call these sniper attacks.

If people want to stay in the background, remain anonymous, and take shots at the leaders and the church, they are snipers. They should not have a voice if they are not willing to be known. If we let one person speak on behalf of unnamed other people, we are encouraging sniper attacks.

Another problem with allowing one person to speak for a whole group of anonymous people is that we have no idea if these people really exist. We also have no way of knowing if the words brought by this spokesperson really reflect the feelings of the "unnamed people."

Through my years of ministry, I have never allowed a person to speak on behalf of an unknown group of dissenters. I won't even let board members or pastors bring a message from other people or a group. If someone wants to share a concern, they should come and share it prayerfully, gracefully, and personally.

If they will not show their face, but still want to criticize, they are snipers.

For the same reason, I never read an unsigned letter. I throw them away. If a letter is addressed to a staff member, the board, or to me, but it is not signed, it will not be read.

The one exception is if someone sends an unsigned letter that I can tell at a glance is complimentary, then I will break the rule and read the letter over and over!

5. Pray for humility.

When someone has the courage to come, face-to-face, and share their concerns, listen. Pray for humility and open your ears. Listening does not mean you agree. But it does honor those who take the time to come and share their hearts. If they have avoided the temptation to be a sniper and want to talk, keep your door, ears, and heart open.

Over the years I have learned that there is almost always something to be learned from these encounters. If a person has helpful insight and seeks to communicate with grace, there is a good chance they will be working at your side for the U-Turn vision sooner rather than later. If they come across mean and spiteful, there still might be something helpful in their words. Look for it. And if there is nothing helpful and they are simply angry and on the attack, see number 3 on this list (the value of apathy).

6. Seek wise counsel.

During the years of leading a U-Turn at Corinth Church, there were times when I would begin to feel hurt or discouraged. On a number of those occasions I called my friend Bob Bouwer. He is a man of great wisdom and passion. I would seek his counsel. I would listen to his insights. And I would receive encouragement from him.

At other times I would join with a small group of pastors who were seeking to lead dynamic and transformational churches. Their counsel and hope-filled encouragement would spur me on. In the tough times, read great books that fortify your soul and prepare you to press on. You can also find a person who is part of a church that is farther down the road on their U-Turn adventure and let them cheer you on. Don't travel alone; seek wise counsel.

7. Remember that you are in good company.

Through my years as a follower of Jesus, I have often thought about what I might ask various Bible characters if I could meet them face-to-face and have a private conversation. If I could talk with the apostle Paul, I would say, "Can I see your back?"

Why would I ask this?

Because Paul had 195 scars on his back. Paul told the church at Corinth that he had been restrained on five occasions and had received the forty lashes less one. Five times the apostle Paul had been beaten within an inch of his life.[3]

I can't imagine what went through his mind the fifth time they restrained him. These beatings came not because Paul was rebellious to God or disobedient to the Father's will. His scourging came because he was faithful, because he preached the gospel, and because he was following Jesus.

When you are pushing forward in God's call to be a U-Turn church, don't be surprised when you face resistance. Don't be shocked that there are battles along the way. Don't give up. Don't become hardhearted; stay soft.

Remember that Jesus went to the cross for broken and sinful people. Don't forget that there was not a single inch on Paul's back that was not scarred. The apostle Paul told his young apprentice, Timothy, "Everyone who wants to live a godly life in Christ Jesus will be persecuted."[4]

The question is not whether we will face painful moments on the U-Turn road. The real issue is, when we face these times, can we keep a tender heart?

U-Turn Exercises and Activities

U-Turn Exercise—Listen Up

If there are those in your church who have been trying to express their concerns but no one seems to be listening, take the time to hear them out. Invite them to share what is on their hearts in a healthy and prayerful way. Learn what you can from them, pray for them, and thank them for caring enough about the church to speak up.

U-Turn Exercise—Getting Prayerfully Apathetic

Identify one person who is resisting and trying to block the U-Turn in your church. Commit to do two things in the coming week. First, pray that God will open his heart and change his attitude. Second, pray for a heavenly apathy. Ask God to take care of him and to free you from feeling discouraged and down about his behavior.

U-Turn Reflection Questions

Gather with some leaders and key influencers from your church, read this chapter, ahead of time or together, and talk about the following questions:

- How can we keep inviting people into the U-Turn process? In particular, how can we build natural on-ramps for people who might be late adopters and could be ready to join in, if asked?
- Do we encourage snipers and give room for "unnamed people" to sway the direction of the church? How can we stop sniper attacks in our church?
- Who do you go to for wise counsel and insight?

U-Turn Prayers

Gather with church friends, leaders, or small-group members and pray in the following directions:

- Ask God to help you keep your eyes on Jesus as you press forward with your U-Turn.
- Pray for wisdom to know when you should listen to dissent and concerns. Ask God to help you know when you should take a stance of apathy toward someone who continues to attack and stir things up in the church.
- Lift up those people who are struggling with your church's new direction. Ask God to soften their hearts, open their ears, and help them see the vision He has given your church.

9

Taking Holy Risks

by Bob Bouwer

There are places in this world that are safe, tame, and predictable . . .
helping lead a U-Turn in your church is not one of these places.

When I look back on the story of Faith Church, which is almost fifty years old now, I see a church built by really good people. Yet when I first arrived, there was agreement across the board that we were a comfortable church, we were declining, and we wanted to turn things around. We admitted that even our risk-taking was always comfortable. The risks we took to expand the kingdom of God were always safe.

To experience a U-Turn requires more than taking safe and comfortable risks; it takes uncomfortable holy risks. What is a holy risk? It is a movement or a step forward into the future that requires tremendous faith in God. If there is nothing else that you walk away with in this chapter, remember that. It's the belief that God is the only one who could accomplish the task that is before us. Most churches that are struggling would have to admit to themselves that their risk required little faith, few resources, few prayers, and little sacrifice. But the uncomfortable, holy risk requires God-sized faith, God-sized prayer, and God-sized sacrifice that can become very uncomfortable. Webster's defines risk as a "possibility of loss or injury." These sacrifices could be financial or they could involve time. To accomplish a certain task, it may require extra personal time and energy that you aren't sure you're ready to give up. As Christians, we are called to be bold and step out of our comfort zone.[1] In Matthew 14, Jesus, walking on the water in a storm, summons Peter to come to Him on the water. Jesus said, "*Take courage! It is I. Don't be afraid,*" and tells Peter to step out of his comfort zone. Peter was comfortable in his boat, not attempting to do something he knew he couldn't do in his own power. Yet he took the risk, trusting Jesus to help him.

When I first joined Faith Church serving as a co-pastor, I spent time getting to know the people, loving them, and praying and wrestling about the future. When I became the senior pastor, I asked the consistory what we wanted to look like, what we wanted Faith Church to be about. It was unanimous that we all wanted to see Faith Church turn around. We wanted to see the young people in our church stay in the church. We wanted to see people who were far from God become alive in Jesus Christ. We knew this was God's will, and when it's God's will, He will bless it. We wanted to make the changes necessary. However, whenever we talked about specific changes, we started to have some kickback. We chose to go on a weekend retreat to focus. At the close of that retreat we all agreed that we needed to take a risk. We were ready to get out of the boat.

Holy Risk #1: Second Service

The biggest risk was to offer a new worship style. The year was 1993, and a group of leaders came together to discuss a different worship experience. We decided to offer the new style of worship in October 1994. I remember taking a deep sigh and saying, "Whew! That gives me twelve months to continue with the status quo." Throughout the year, I began to realize that things were going to change, and I didn't know how the congregation would react. An elder offered to lead the movement toward the new style in worship. The first startling moment was when he said from the pulpit that Faith

Church was going to offer a new experience in worship. He explained that we would have our normal traditional service at 9:30 a.m., but we would offer a new style of worship at 11:15 a.m. Hearing the announcement increased my awareness that we were about to take an enormous risk. I remembered all the fears associated with the door hangers we hung in the surrounding communities. I remember saying to myself, *I just hope one person shows up.* We laid a lot on the line. We took a tremendous risk.

Walking into that first service, seeing about one hundred sixty people, I learned a valuable lesson about God's will. I learned about the power of holy risk. When you do something that you feel is God's will, something that is beyond you and me, something only God could accomplish, you have the confidence to continue.

Holy Risk #2: Third Service

I started to realize that a pattern was being established. Once we took a big step, there was the confidence to take the next one. The next big move was to add another service on Sunday mornings after our contemporary service grew too large to accommodate everyone that attended it. We started the traditional service early, followed by two back-to-back contemporary services.

Holy Risk #3: Single Focus

As we continued to grow, one of our leaders made the bold motion at a board meeting to become a single-focused church. He presented the idea of eliminating our traditional worship service and going solely with the contemporary style. We would simply say this is who we are, unashamed, take it or leave it.

I remember thinking the decision our board was about to make would be a holy risk because I knew it would cause many in our church to consider leaving. Consequently, about sixty-five people did leave. But we felt the risk was worth it. The people who left joined a church more to their liking. New people that joined were becoming connected to Christ for the very first time, or reconnected after years of being away from the church.

I think of the story of Gideon (Judges 7), when the Lord brought his army down to just a few. Gideon took a holy risk, sensing by faith that this downsizing was for the greater good.

Holy Risk #4: Fourth Service

Within months, all three services became packed. We learned from our conferences and studies along the way that if a visitor walks into a church that is packed, chances are they will not return, and they may even turn around and leave. We were told that you must always have enough empty seats so a visitor doesn't feel they are taking someone else's seat. Empty seats imply that you have room for them. Eventually our slogan on a billboard advertisement along the highway became "We're saving a seat for you."

To help with the overcrowding, we decided to add a Saturday night service, and again it was a kind of holy risk. We didn't know if it would break up the feeling of unity that we were experiencing. We were risking the feel of a separate church. Once again, our risk proved fruitful. We intentionally would state that there were four services, but only one church. The unity wasn't crushed, and the people kept coming.

Holy Risk #5: Building in Indiana

The holy risks we took are still bearing fruit. We started asking what we were going to do next. We had four services in a small A-frame sanctuary that seated about two hundred seventy-five comfortably. A group of leaders spent months and months studying options and praying. One evening, we gathered many of the leaders together at an off-site location and spent about three hours in prayer. We broke up into several groups to pray and then came together to discuss our options. Every group came back with the same prompting. They all felt the Lord was challenging us to relocate to Indiana (not far from our Illinois location). We confidently shared with the congregation our plan to relocate to Indiana.

A financial campaign was launched and $4.2 million was raised. The only problem was that the building we needed would cost $9.6 million.

One of our elders said to the board that $4.2 million was comfortable, but $9.6 million required faith. We unanimously made the decision to take the risk. Again I thank God, because 900 people committed to $4.2 million, and our numbers increased to 2,800 in about eighteen months! The fruit of our holy risk.

I think of Abraham, who by faith left his comfortable home and all that he knew and set out for a land that God would show him.[2]

Holy Risk #6: Multi-Sites

After purchasing land and completing the church, we were thrilled to have a worship center that would hold about four times the number of people as our old building. Yet within two years, we were bursting at the seams again! We never have had the attitude that "we're big enough," because we knew that every single soul that walked through our doors mattered to God. If God continued to bring people in, we would continue to make room for them. We started with Band-Aid moves, such as knocking down an exterior wall of our brand-new building to make more room in our atrium. Then we added the "Garage," a space designed for youth, and put a basketball court outside. We added classrooms and meeting rooms. These Band-Aid moves did not require a huge risk. As we continued to grow, we realized that we needed a God-sized risk once more.

We hired a consultant, who studied our church situation and came back with a huge report. He said that we needed to get more seats, and quickly. He suggested that we embrace the multi-site movement. We didn't even know what that meant. He explained that you find another space, such as a high school gym, and present a live worship experience with band and singers. You have a campus pastor and a live children's ministry going on, but the message is a live recording of the service back at the Dyer site, projected on a video screen. Again, we were faced with a holy risk.

I wondered at the time if this would work. Would people really show up to watch a video recording of a sermon? I had my doubts, and fears. Someone said, "Here we go again. It's another holy risk." And I was reminded of the fruit from the risks we took in the past. We began repeating the phrase "one church, multiple locations" to let the congregation know that we were not planting a separate church. We took the leap of faith, and now more than three hundred fifty people are worshiping in Cedar Lake, Indiana, about eleven miles southeast of our campus.

As I mentioned earlier, we were approached by a church in Valparaiso, close to forty-five minutes away. They were dying, down in attendance to about twenty. After much prayer, we stepped out of the boat once more. In the midst of a recession, we purchased the building for $1.2 million, and more than a hundred people now worship at Valparaiso.

I have also mentioned the group of people worshiping in Sheridan, Illinois, an hour and forty-five minutes away. They asked if they could take our DVD and start a worship service in a barn. Currently more than sixty worship there, many of whom are new believers. One family took a risk.

We are praying and considering new and different multi-sites. Our most recent campus has been added in Hammond, Indiana, where a core group committed to launch this site. This is a new holy risk because we are moving into a multicultural and diverse social economic community. Sitting in a circle of brothers and sisters in Christ, dreaming with the framework of a holy risk before us, has become a delight. I hope and pray that Faith Church will never stop taking holy risks.

Holy Risk #7: The Ravines

Several years ago an idea came to me and our leaders to create a marriage hospital. It would be a place where couples struggling with their marriage, some fallen into deep sin or financial ruin, could stay in-residence for three- five- or seven-day intensive therapy. We took the risk. We decided it was something God was calling us to do. We didn't have a facility for this, but God provided through a family who donated a house and property. In 2009, we opened *The Ravines* for any Christian couple who has fallen into any kind of difficulty in their marriage. We've seen couples come in complete brokenness and watched God bring incredible healing.

Do you remember the story of Joshua leading the Israelites at God's command into the land He had promised them? As soon as the priests carrying the ark of the covenant stepped into the swollen Jordan River, a miracle happened and the waters parted before them. Joshua and his elders took a risk, trusting God even when they could not see the results ahead of time.

To understand holy risk, we must understand God's part in it. The Bible teaches us that God knows all things, He is omniscient; there is nothing outside His knowledge. With God there is no risk; He knows everything. He knows the outcome before it happens.

But we do not know all things. In fact, we know very little. Most of our lives require risk because we don't know what's ahead. We take risks every day. When you drive over a bridge spanning a deep ravine or a river, do you ever think about the risk? How about financial investments in the stock market or real estate? Those are real risks. You take a risk every time you get into your car, every time you go through an intersection. The light is green for you, but will the person who has the red light stop? Every time you board an airplane you are taking a risk. All of life is a risk, but when it comes to moving ahead in our churches, we often don't want to take a risk. Matthew 6:30 says, *"O you of little faith."* God is challenging His church to take holy risks. A holy risk involves any movement that goes beyond our human comfort zone, beyond our human means, beyond our natural capabilities. I've learned over the years that when churches say they are willing to take a risk, they are usually referring to a safe risk, when in reality a holy risk is required. Churches that turn around are churches that take holy risks.

Principles of Holy Risk

Over the last twenty years at Faith Church, I've been able to look back and reflect on the key principles for our taking holy risks.

Principle #1: Sharing the Vision

The first principle of holy risk is that God will prompt the pastor and/ or elders about the possibility of taking such a risk. Someone has to step up to the plate and say, "I have a dream" or "I have a thought." God prompts; the leader plants the seed.

At Faith Church, we have an annual event called Vision Retreat. We take key leaders and their spouses away for a weekend. We worship the Lord, we fellowship together, and we look back on the things God has enabled us to accomplish in the last year. The vast majority of the weekend is spent looking ahead and asking what it is that God wants us to do next.

We will often share an idea, a vision, or a prompting of what God might have for us. I am not the only one who gets these leadings from the Lord. We work as a team. I depend on that. Together we ask the Lord to bring clarity, which usually ends up requiring a risk of some kind. I want to give a word of warning here: The Lord works in community, in His body, so be careful of the individual who says, "The Lord told me that we must do this" when no one else affirms it. Yes, the Lord may prompt one leader, but the body of Christ together owns it and affirms it.

After the Lord prompts a leader, the next move is to bring it out into concentric leadership circles. For us it would be the management team, the elders, the deacons, the consistory board of our church, and finally to the entire congregation. At each step it is critical to keep motives in check. Are they pure? Are they in line with what God is saying to all your leaders?

Principle #2: Prayer

The second principle is prayer. There can be no forward movement in a holy risk without a tremendous amount of prayer.

John Calvin said, "Prayer is a communication between God and us whereby we expound to Him our desires, our joys, our sighs, in a word, all the thoughts in our hearts."[3] He also said that prayer is where we are "permitted to pour into God's bosom the difficulties which torment us in order that He may loosen the knots which we cannot untie."[4]

Part of taking a holy risk is speaking to God, asking if it is not from Him, that He would close the door. If it is from God, we ask for the boldness and confidence necessary to take the risk. At Faith Church, we became clearly aware that the more we prayed, the more confident and willing we became. I cannot stress enough the importance of prayer.

Principle #3: Biblically In-Line

The third principle is to verify the possibility of the holy risk, looking at all the components to be sure each one is biblical. Can it be backed up with Scripture? Will it expand the kingdom of God? Are there any parts of it that don't match with what the Scriptures teach?

When checking out the multi-site option, we asked the question: Is having multi-sites biblical? The book of Acts tells the story of the multiplying church, preaching in various cities, and meeting in various homes. What about offering a DVD message and a campus pastor? We wrestled with these issues. Our goal has always been for each campus to have its own autonomy, not identical, but identifiable. We use our own preaching staff, offering live preaching twice a month. We hold close to what Scripture says about the local church body.

Principle #4: Logic

The fourth principle is logic. God has given us His Word, the vehicle of prayer, and His Holy Spirit to prompt us and lead us. He also gave us a brain. Logic plays into taking risks.

At a Leadership Summit at Willow Creek many years ago, we heard that in a group of people, no matter what the number, 100, 200, or 10,000, the dynamics will be the same. Two percent of the people will always say no to an idea. Two percent will always say yes. Ten percent will lean toward no; 10 percent will lean toward yes. Then there will always be about 75 percent who will go with the leader's decision. No matter what the issue, no matter what the size of the group, these statistics have held true. It was comforting to know that more than likely about 75 percent of the people were going to be with me and with our board. In our experience, these group dynamic statistics have been correct with the risks that we presented to the congregation.

A couple of years ago, we came to the point where we needed to expand again at our Dyer campus. We hired an architect, who created a blueprint and model for a 3,000-seat auditorium. It was absolutely beautiful. It looked like a great fit for us. When the architects brought us their proposal, we were at the beginning of the recession. We sat down and decided together that we needed to wait. We didn't want to risk a $20 million investment in the midst of a recession that could bring us to our financial knees. It may have been a God-sized risk, but that doesn't mean it was *from* God. For us, logic prevailed.

Even when we use our heads, our consultants' heads, and all the knowledge available to us, a decision isn't always crystal clear. At those times we have to use our hearts as well. We have to humbly seek God's direction through prayer, searching the Scriptures, and being alert to the Holy Spirit's prompting. If our actions aren't right, we will know by the fruit. If we are on the right path, we will see movement of the gospel, life change, and conversion.

Principle #5: Faith

The fifth principle of holy risk-taking is the element of faith. Faith is where you bring together the logic, the prayers, the Scripture-backing, the leadings from the Lord, and then you ask yourself the question, "Is this a God-sized risk or is it a human-sized risk?" I think a holy risk is God-sized. I don't know what that means to your specific church situation, but whatever that is, it has to be one step beyond what you could accomplish alone. There's no doubt that a holy risk could result in failure. We can trust our sovereign God that even though by human standards we may have failed, by divine standards we have still won because failure shapes us. I've made many mistakes in ministry. I've taken some risks that have not turned out as I would have liked them to. And I'll tell you, I'm a better person because of it. I've learned a lot about myself and a lot about leadership. So yes, you could fail, but ultimately you win because God is with you and redeems the situation.

I love to challenge myself to things I cannot do, that only God can do. Those are the risks that require faith.

Principle #6: Decision-Making

The sixth principle is making the decision. We pray, we look at the logic, we do our wrestling in prayer, but at some point we have to pull the trigger. We often say those exact words: "Are we ready to pull the trigger?"

There is power in decision. Often churches will get stuck in the worry, the waiting, the indecision, and they end up doing nothing. Making a decision gets things moving.

Principle #7: Communication

The seventh principle is communication to the congregation. Faith Church is led by a consistory board. When our consistory made the decision to relocate, the congregation was informed. They didn't vote on it; they were informed about it and were asked for their support. Communication to the congregation about a decision the leaders have made is crucial. Present a future that is bright. Ask them to join with you, to be united, and then take questions to help them understand. We try to educate the congregation about the history of the decision, but the communication comes after the decision is made. It would not work for the entire congregation to go through the principles of a holy risk.

Just as Joshua received the word of the Lord about crossing the Jordan, and then shared with the Israelites that it was time to cross the river, in the same way, church leaders receive the word or the calling to move forward and then inform their people, counting on their faith and trust to follow.

Principle #8: Celebration

The eighth principle is to celebrate. First, we celebrated what God was going to do. When we were still in the old building but had made the decision to relocate, we had Celebration Sunday. We rented a hall and had a formal dinner, inviting the entire congregation to celebrate with us what God was going to do. We celebrated having made the decision, and then began our fundraising with the dinner. We had no idea at that point *what* God was going to do, but we celebrated our moving forward.

Two years after we relocated, we had a service where we invited those who had come alive in Christ within the last couple of years to stand up. About 65 percent of the congregation stood. It was exciting. We clapped and we celebrated because of what God had done.

Holy-Risk Churches

When it comes to the various kinds of churches, I like to use this analogy: There is the undertaker church, the caretaker church, and the risk-taking church. The undertaker church is on the way to burying itself. They look back and they have pictures of the past but no plans for the future. The caretaker church is the one that says, "We don't want to do anything; we just want to maintain our church as it is." Their goal is to keep the fortress and the walls up and keep the people they have. The risk-taking church is the one that has the faith in God to step out and bear fruit for the kingdom of God.

Faith Church is experiencing the fruit of holy risk-taking. More than three thousand people have joined our church. Close to 65 percent of them became members as new believers. A large portion of the remaining 35 percent are people who were stuck in other churches that weren't growing, and they came to Faith Church to become who they could be in Christ.

The kingdom of God needs churches that are willing to take risks. Missionaries all over the world are risking their lives to reach the lost, yet we often hold back when we have so much less at stake.

- The average Christian church in America has seventy-five members.
- In America, 80 to 85 percent of all churches have either reached a plateau or have declined.
- America is the fourth most unchurched nation on earth.

What is the Lord asking you to do that requires risk? What would it take for you to move beyond what is comfortable and be involved in something that only God could accomplish? What may the Lord be prompting your church to do in order to move forward? If you were assured that you couldn't fail, what would you like to do for the kingdom in your church? Remember, some visions start with a dream.

I hope and pray that you and your church, individually and collectively in your walk with the Lord, will wrestle with what holy risks the Lord has in mind for you.

Kevin's Reflections on Taking Holy Risks

After reading this chapter you might be saying to yourself, *Taking risks is easy for Bob. He is one of those tough-hearted leaders who will press forward no matter what others might think. He must be a risk-taker by nature.*

It would be easy to come to that kind of a conclusion after reading about a church that has taken so many risks over the past decade. It might even be a reasonable conclusion to reach if you have never met Bob Bouwer face-to-face.

Let me tell you the truth of the matter. Bob is a pastor at heart. He loves people. In the midst of leading a large, growing, and dynamic church ministry, he has stayed tender toward God, humble before people, and willing to take risks, even when they stretch his faith.

If you are a leader who is sensitive about hurting church members as you move forward, if you are a person who loves the church and wants to keep peace in the family, if you have a tenderhearted temperament and have an aversion to stepping on people's toes, you are not alone. Many U-Turn leaders are wired just like you. As a matter of fact, one of the ways Bob Bouwer and I are dramatically different is that he is far more sensitive, tenderhearted, and pastoral than I am.

I share this because I want pastors and leaders to know that God can use all kinds of personalities to help a church move forward and take holy risks. If you think you lack the aggressive nature needed to keep pressing on, taking risks, and calling people to U-Turn action, be assured that God can supply all you need in this department.

As I read this chapter on taking holy risks, I had one distinct risk area that kept coming to mind. Right in the middle of Corinth Church's U-Turn, we decided to plant another church. It did not really make sense from a human perspective. It would demand time, energy, money, and giving up a core of gifted people. It would be a holy risk!

The problem was, we knew God was calling us to begin multiplying. It was time to give away some of the good gifts God had given us. So we brought in a church planter, mentored him, gathered a core of people, and launched Wayfarer Community Church. This whole process took more than a year.

When the core group was launched, the risky nature of this decision became even more apparent. Half of our drummers went on to the church plant. Many of our high school youth ministry volunteers went. Some dear friends were part of the new work. And in addition to our commitment to financially support the new church, those who went on the plant began giving to Wayfarer.

We anticipated some of the consequences of taking this holy risk, but others surprised us. There was sacrifice involved on many levels. It cost us to take this step and follow God's leading.

There was also inexpressible joy in being part of this birthing process. There was pride in watching our daughter church grow and begin reaching out. When I got to stand and help serve the bread and cup at the first Communion service of this new ministry, I was overwhelmed!

As an addendum, with time, God replenished all the people we sent on the church plant. After months of praying, in just one week God sent us two new drummers. New families kept coming and new volunteers stepped up to serve with the youth. We discovered that there is always a cost to taking a holy risk. If there were no cost, it would not be a risk. At the same time, there is also amazing blessing in following God into His dreams and visions, no matter how risky they might be.

U-Turn Exercises and Activities

U-Turn Exercise

Identify a single holy risk that you personally or your church could take. Go through the first five holy risk principles with that risk in mind.

1. Sharing the Vision: Have you shared your vision with other leaders?
2. Prayer: Have you prayed about it?
3. Biblically In-Line: Is your vision in line with Scripture?
4. Logic: Is your vision a logical risk?
5. Faith: Does your vision involve a God-sized risk or a human-sized risk?

After applying these five principles, if you still feel led to continue on with your holy risk, consider going through the principles with a group of leaders and then walk through the remaining three principles:

6. Decision-Making
7. Communication
8. Celebration

U-Turn Reflection Questions

1. What are the possible losses or sacrifices that you most fear?
2. What new thing did you learn from this chapter?
3. On a scale of 1 to 5, where would you put yourself as a holy risk-taker and where would you put your church?

|—————————————————————————————|

| 1 | 2 | 3 | 4 | 5 |

Low Holy   High Holy
Risk-Taker   Risk-Taker

10

Looking Out

by Kevin G. Harney

The gravitational force of the church naturally pulls us inward,
toward each other.
If we are going to move outward toward those who are lost,
it will take more energy than most of us dream.

Once a month, during the elders' meeting, someone would poke their head out the door at around seven-thirty to see if anyone was standing in the hall waiting to make a "public profession of faith." If someone was there, they were invited in. This was how we received new members at Corinth Church when I first became the pastor. It was the way things had been done for about a hundred years.

An announcement was printed in the bulletin the previous Sunday, letting the congregation know anyone was welcome to come to the church on Tuesday evening if they wanted to make a public declaration of faith in Jesus, if they wanted to reaffirm their faith in the Savior, or if they wanted to request baptism.

If someone came to make a confession of their faith, they would sit with the entire board of elders and share their testimony. Then there would be an open time when the pastors and elders could ask questions about the person's beliefs, faith, and personal spiritual journey. It was always a very exciting and positive evening when someone would publically express faith in Jesus before the leaders of the church.

Most months no one would come. We didn't really expect anyone to be out in the hall at seven-thirty. But we were glad when someone did show up.

Turn the clock ahead five or six years into our U-Turn process.

It was a very different scenario. We had a sign-up sheet where people would put their name and request to meet with the elders a few weeks in advance of the monthly meeting. Then we would begin calling all the elders who were serving presently and also those who had served any time in the past fifty years. We gathered every elder we could find. We had a host greet the individuals as they came to meet with the elders. Refreshments were served. It was a party!

We would pair up pastors, elders, and other church leaders and make sure there were enough pairs to meet with all those requesting to come to the meeting on Tuesday night.

Instead of meeting in my office, as we had done when we began our U-Turn, we met in the church gym. I remember times when we stood in a circle to do introductions and have an opening prayer, and the circle was the size of the basketball court. I remember elders who had served many years before, walking into the gym to help us receive new members and having their breath taken away when they saw all the people. We would send a pair of leaders with a person or family so they could sit with these folks and hear their story of faith.

If these past church leaders had any residue of resistance to the new church direction, it melted away in these holy moments. As they listened to testimonies and prayed with these fresh new Christians, something amazing happened.

I remember the tears in the eyes of these faithful leaders when they heard the stories of changed lives, conversions, and the manifest presence of God breaking into lives, marriages, and families. When they would come back to the elders and give a report about the conversion of a high school student who grew up in a non-believing home, they were overwhelmed. When they reported on the brand-new faith of a single mom struggling to raise three little ones, they were no longer resisting outreach . . . they were asking how we could do more to reach people who needed what only Jesus could give. When they came back and told us about a couple who had met Jesus through the ministry of Corinth and were seeking to restore their broken marriage, these leaders became the greatest ambassadors of being a U-Turn church. As more and more people bowed their knees to Jesus and surrendered their lives, attitudes changed.

I am convinced that these moments were not only sacred to the heart of God, but they became holy ground for our leaders. Some of these members of the "greater board of elders," had gone years without hearing a testimony of faith in Jesus, and now they were hearing them every month. They were seeing that our U-Turn was not about music style, the number of services, the need for more staff, or any of the dozens of other issues we faced along the way. It was about more and more people coming to know and love Jesus.

The transformation of the way we received new members became a snapshot of the deeper spiritual reality. The revival and renewal that faithful saints had prayed for over the previous decades was now breaking into the daily life of the church. Souls were being saved. Families were coming, not just to church, but to Jesus! This ever-present and growing reality propelled us forward.

Those who had resisted the U-Turn for years began to get it. They might not have liked some of the new things and changes we had introduced, but they loved God and they loved people. As more and more came to embrace Jesus as the forgiver of their sins and the Lord of their life, church members became converts to the idea of being a U-Turn church.

The DNA of a U-Turn Church

By now you have discovered that the DNA of a U-Turn church is saturated with a commitment to evangelistic outreach. Both Faith Church and Corinth Church began seeing a growing number of people come to a real and life-giving relationship with Jesus. Both Bob and I continued to raise the banner of outreach in every area of the church ministry.

If you dropped in for a visit to either Faith or Corinth Church today, you would feel it in the air. You can see it in every ministry. These churches have sacrificed, paid the price, and given up much because of a confident belief in the gospel and an undying love for people. The hearts of these churches beat with the heart of God. They are about more than taking care of those who already know Jesus . . . they are about looking outward.

Both Faith Church and Corinth Church have made a commitment to reaching out on every level of church life. We have discovered that evangelism does not just happen. It takes commitment and energy. It takes strategy and funding. It takes relentless love and consistent prayer. With time, it becomes so much a part of the church DNA that the idea of not reaching out feels ungodly and profane.

I am so committed to outreach that I could make this chapter hundreds of pages long . . . but we don't have room for that. In fact, I have written three books on evangelism: One is about personal evangelism, one is about church outreach, and the third is about making your home a lighthouse of God's grace.[1] What I will do in the space I have is give a handful of core ideas that will help your church begin the process of making outreach part of the fabric and DNA of your congregation.

Helping Your Church Look Outward

1. Outreach is for everyone.

One way to move forward in being an outreach-focused church is to grow in your understanding that evangelism is not an occasional activity reserved for a select group of gifted people. Evangelism is for every person who has faith in Jesus Christ. Jesus was clear that we are to be His light in a dark world and salt on this earth. Our lives should cause people to thirst for the living water of Jesus.[2] Peter exhorts us to *"be prepared to give an answer to everyone who asks you to give the reason for the hope that you have. But do this with gentleness and respect."*[3]

A U-Turn church calls everyone to learn how to share their story of faith and God's message of redemption. When a church with sixty-five people has sixty-five witnesses to the love of God and saving power of Jesus, things start to turn around! Even a small church becomes an unstoppable force when everyone understands that they can serve in the name of Jesus, love with the grace of Jesus, and share the life-saving gospel of Jesus.

This dream will become a reality as it is preached from the pulpit, over and over. It will infiltrate the culture of the church as each ministry leader believes they are leading an outreach movement and not just a children's ministry, youth group, college Bible study, women's ministry, or some other specific program. Outreach will become the lifeblood of a church when the Great Commission becomes as important to us as it is to the Savior whose name we bear: *"Therefore go and make disciples of all nations, baptizing them in the name of the Father and of the Son and of the Holy Spirit, and teaching them to obey everything I have commanded you. And surely I am with you always, to the very end of the age."*[4]

2. Outreach is about the whole church.

As we embrace the truth that every believer carries the good news in their heart and on their lips, a church begins to change. Outreach is not seen as a quarterly or yearly excursion to some remote place where we perform a religious duty and then check that off our list until the next official event. Evangelism becomes a lifestyle, and the whole church becomes a missionary movement right in the community where God has planted it.

This means we might have an outreach team or planning group for special events, but every single ministry of the church begins to pray and plan for outreach. The men's ministry begins to ask how they might share God's love with unbelieving men in their community. The women's ministry is no longer content having programs that are designed to meet their needs and make them happy. They begin planning gatherings that would be a natural entry point for women who still need to meet Jesus face-to-face. The people who lead the children's ministry realize that the church is not a place to hide their good little children from a scary world. Instead, it is a place to invite other kids who might be different and even difficult. Every ministry of the church begins to say, "We are about outreach!"

Part of this happens when hearts are changed and leaders (both volunteer and staff) long to see lost sheep come home to their loving Shepherd.[5] It also happens when we create lines of accountability for all of our ministry leaders. A U-Turn church will appoint leaders who have a heart for outreach and will even remove leaders who refuse to reach out beyond the sheep that are already in the fold. Evangelism is that important to the heart of God and it should be that critical to us.

3. Train, train, and then . . . train some more.

One way to make sure the vision for outreach continues to grow and does not fizzle out is to do regular training. This should not be a voluntary class offered once or twice a year for those who want to come. It should be part of the fabric of every ministry in the church.

Actually, the best place for this training is from the pulpit. At least once a year, every pastor should do a series on God's love for the world and our call to reach out. There are great resources to help keep this training fresh and powerful.[6]

Along with church-wide training, every ministry in the church can have their own outreach training events that are shaped to reach people in their particular area of ministry focus. The way we reach children can be quite different from how we do evangelism to college students. A U-Turn church will customize training in outreach for the various ministries in the church and make sure there is a time for equipping at least once a year.

4. Tune in to the presence of the spiritually disconnected.

Every time we gather for worship, we should be aware that there are people present who do not know Jesus. They are searching, seeking, and curious. But they are not yet part of God's family . . . they are disconnected. We should do our ministry with a deep level of sensitivity to these people. We need to be sure we do not use "insider language" and assume a high level of spiritual understanding.

Since I grew up in a non-believing, non-church-attending home, this is always on the front burner of my mind. I am always thinking about how a spiritually disconnected person would feel when they are with us. This does not mean we should avoid passionate worship and deep teaching of the Word in our worship services. What it does mean is that we need to use vocabulary that will connect with the uninitiated. We must not make people feel like outsiders, or worse . . . stupid!

I remember one Sunday, early in my time at Corinth, when a song leader decided to add a "familiar worship song" to the worship set . . . on the spur of the moment. He looked over at the piano player and said, "Let's just do a verse or two of one of my favorite songs, 'I'm So Glad I'm a Part of the Family of God.'" The pianist started playing and the song leader said these fateful words, "I'm sure all of you know this one." Then he began singing. There was no hymn number announced, no words on a screen, and no help for a person who was visiting and unfamiliar with the words to the song.

I tried to focus on worship, but found my heart going out to those people who were standing there . . . not singing . . . feeling awkward . . . feeling like outsiders . . . maybe even feeling stupid!

This led to a number of conversations and efforts to make sure that our worship services and church ministries were always tuned in to those present who that had no spiritual heritage to lean upon. Up to this point, the church members would occasionally recite the Lord's Prayer or the Apostle's Creed from memory. We did not stop using these, but we did make sure they were printed so people could participate if they wanted to. Sometimes we forgot to think of those who were visiting and unaware of our traditions and insider practices. But by God's grace, and with careful planning, we worked to include these people as much as we could.

A U-Turn church tunes in to the fact that there are always people among us that are still on their journey toward Jesus. We think of them. We love them. We will even tailor what we do to make sure their needs are met. If we no longer have to worry about being sensitive to visitors because everyone at our church is already a believer, then we have an even greater problem!

One of the challenges we faced at Corinth Church, and that I now address at Shoreline Church, is the issue of how we conduct our worship services. Some congregations have moved away from inviting people into deep and personal worship. They feel this will make visitors and spiritual seekers uncomfortable.

I disagree.

I have always been a proponent of keeping the focus on worship and not entertainment. Some years ago, Sally Morgenthaler wrote a book called *Worship Evangelism*.[7] In a nutshell, the book claims that believers should engage in authentic and passionate worship, and that this will become an attractive model for those who are not yet following Jesus. The key is that we create a safe place for believers to worship and seekers to engage at whatever level they are comfortable.

5. Use the power of stories.

Another way to grow the passion and commitment for outreach in your church is by telling stories of God's transforming power. These testimonies will inspire those whose hearts have grown cold. They will also help your church members see that their service and sacrifice are making an eternal difference.

A testimony or story of faith is not only an account of how someone became a follower of Jesus, although, of course, this is important. It is also a time when people tell about how God is using them now to share the love and message of Jesus with others. It could also be an account of how God has moved in someone's life and done something powerful, amazing, or unusual.

In a U-Turn church, stories are very important. God is on the move, and we need to let people know about what He is doing. If you can have a testimony every Sunday, it is not too often. I know that Rick Warren, at Saddleback Church, tries to have at least one story of faith in every worship service. It is a normal part of His message.

Testimonies can be live, with a person standing up and telling about their conversion or how God is moving in their life. It can be recorded and played during a worship service. It can be written down and included in a service bulletin or on a Web site. You can have children and youth tell their stories. Couples and singles can share about how God is alive in their lives. Be creative, be consistent, and make a commitment to glorify God and inspire your congregation through stories of faith.

6. Try stuff and be creative.

When it comes to reaching out, I give people this important piece of advice, *Try something!* Too many believers and churches sit around hoping people will come and visit their church. Many Christians are afraid to be innovative and creative because they are worried their idea won't work or it will not bear fruit. I say, "Give it a try and see what happens!"

As we pressed forward with the U-Turn process at Corinth Church, something amazing began to happen. People came with ideas for reaching out. The Spirit of God birthed passion and dreams. Others heard about something that was working at another church and they came and said, "Can we try this?" In most cases, if they were willing to help lead the new initiative, we said, "Yes!"

One person wanted us to begin going to new people in the community and taking an invitation and a small gift. It turns out you can get a list of new residents through the city. We began a "Bag Ministry," where we would make welcome bags with an invitation, candy, a pen, pencil, a refrigerator magnet (with church information on it), and even a treat for their dog if they had one. Over the coming years, hundreds of people received a personal invitation as teams went out quarterly with these gift bags.

Another person heard about a "Mugging Ministry" where first-time visitors received a follow-up visit from some folks from the church who brought a church coffee mug filled with goodies and literature about the church. This became a great way to care for those who visited and answer any questions they had. It also became an opportunity to have spiritual conversations and share the gospel with those who were interested.

My wife started a yearly Easter Egg Hunt for children in the community, where the gospel was shared before the kids headed out to look for candy-filled eggs. Hundreds and hundreds of children and their parents came to the church campus, had a great time, and heard the story of Easter!

A few years into our U-Turn, a woman came and said, "Could we go to downtown Grand Rapids with a worship team and lead a time of street worship?" I thought this idea was a bit far-fetched, but she was willing to put it together. Over the next few years, teams of worship leaders led times of worship in some of the toughest parts of the city and people loved it! They were drawn to the worship. We ended up bringing food, free books and Bibles, and even free egg-shakers with the church Web address printed on the side. This would allow them to join in the music by adding some percussion with the shaker and have a take-away with church information on it. These services became a powerful tool for outreach in our city.

These are only a few examples of more than fifty different outreach and mission ministries that were birthed as we sought to focus outward. Some worked well and connected with our community. Some did not work. Some lasted a year or two. Others continue to this day. The issue was not worrying if every effort would be successful. What we did was try stuff for Jesus!

If you are wondering where you are in your U-Turn process, one question you can ask is this: "Are we seeing people come to faith in Jesus Christ?" In chapter 2, Bob talked about the importance of numbers in identifying where you are as a church. He looked at the way declining numbers tell a story and can ignite a fresh sense of urgency. In a very similar way, increasing numbers of new believers create a growing commitment to the U-Turn process. When people are coming to the feet of Jesus, repenting, and being radically transformed by His grace, you know that God is on the move!

As I write these words, I am still delighting in a baptism service we had at Shoreline Community Church just a few weeks ago. We planned an outside service at a place called Lovers Point. This is a little cove in the Monterey Bay. The water, on a good day at this time of the year, is frigid. But it was raining and much colder than usual. We were not sure if people would make it out in the bad weather.

We had five pastors standing in the water and rain. That day, forty-one people were baptized in the name of the Father, the Son, and the Holy Spirit. Not only did people show up, but God was clearly there too. Heaven rejoiced, and so did we. A few seals floated about twenty feet from one of the pastors and watched as people were baptized.

I had the distinct feeling that creation was joining in the party!

Bob's Reflections on Looking Out

When Kevin joined our staff as our Teaching Pastor, one of his responsibilities was to increase our outreach (evangelism) temperature. And that he did. He would regularly meet with individuals, departments, and staff, including me, and have us evaluate our outreach temperature. It was a brilliant move. Personally, I began to pray more for the lost and became more intentional about having spiritual conversations with the unchurched. Most people and most churches believe in outreach, but few actually do something about it. "Looking out" can happen in your life and in the life of your church.

As the Lord increased our spiritual temperature at Faith Church, we began to intentionally focus on impacting the local community. Part of that punch came from my Reformed heritage. I remember John Calvin's "U-Turn" impact on Geneva, Switzerland, followed by his impact on the surrounding area, and then his impact literally to the ends of the earth. He and many in his church were involved in the local government and were seated in public office for the purpose of change. They influenced morality, care for the refugees, and much more that changed Geneva. The Reformation church ignited a U-Turn in the city.

In the words of John Calvin, we are the "visible and invisible church."[8] The "invisible" are the called-out people whom God saves. The "visible" church is the church the world sees. God's desire is that the world sees a healthy, united, impacting, and alive church.

U-Turn churches have a worldview that raises people up and urges them to be reformational in sports (e.g., Little League, USA Hockey), business, local government, entertainment, civic responsibilities, and the like. Conducting any and all activities in a Christlike manner gives glory to God.

A turned-around Faith Church is definitely, intentionally impacting our community. We have gone into the school system with the national ministry of Kids Hope USA, a one-on-one mentoring ministry to struggling children. We have witnessed the walls come down in individuals and in the school administration without violating the separation of church and state. We have established a relationship. The public school administration is now using our facility for meetings and training.

The police department came to us and asked if they could train their K-9 dogs at our facility. We not only said yes, but we rolled out the red carpet. Today, all of the surrounding towns and cities come with their drug-sniffing dogs and sniff their way through Faith Church. It is our prayer that they will smell the love of God through a healthy church and our love for them.

We are currently the largest voting center in our town. We contacted city managers and offered our facility for voting. They accepted our offer, and it has been such a blast to host several precincts and see thousands of people flow onto our campus to punch in their votes.

We offer children's events to the community. For a couple of years, we offered Winter Wonderland, our mini-version of what the city of Chicago offered at Navy Pier, during winter break. The facility was filled with inflatable moonwalks, inflatable slides, games, and ice skating outside. We advertised free admission, free food, free drinks, and the place was packed.

On Halloween, Faith Church offers "Trunk or Treat" to the community. It is a safe place for the children to walk from car trunk to car trunk in our parking lot and receive candy. We have games and food as well. With word-of-mouth advertising, we always have a good turnout.

When community people come to an event, they become familiar and comfortable with the facility, which in turn makes them more comfortable checking out a weekend service. Of course, our prayer is that they would come to know the Lord Jesus Christ, and it is important to us that we make the visible church a desirable place.

Our multi-site campus in Cedar Lake has a church-wide community day called Labor of Love. They plant flowers, clean parks, and serve the police and fire departments. It is important to Faith Church that the community knows that we are here to serve them.

So often churches are like a pair of reading glasses. They want the ministry that is close to them to become more in focus without considering the far-sighted vision. U-Turn churches are like bifocals in that the bottom lens focuses up close while the upper lens see more clearly farther out.

How can we continue to be the visible church to our community? That is a question we intentionally keep asking ourselves so that we keep our eyes looking outward toward the broader call of doing whatever we possibly can to share the good news of Jesus Christ. My challenge for you is that you would ask your church to do the same.

U-Turn Exercises and Activities

U-Turn Exercise—Training Time

Review one of the outreach training programs listed in the endnotes of this chapter to see if you can use these resources as tools for training in your church.

U-Turn Exercise—Evaluate a Service

Next time you attend a service of worship at your church, try to listen and watch as if you had never been in a church service in your life. Watch through the eyes of a friend or family member who is not a follower of Jesus. Is there sensitivity to those who are not aware of all the church language and practices? Are there any patterns of practices that would make people feel excluded if they do not have a church background? If you notice anything, share what you learned (with gentleness and humility) with those who could help avoid these things in the future.

U-Turn Reflection Questions

Gather with some leaders and key influencers from your church, read this chapter beforehand, and talk about the following questions:

- Are you seeing people come to faith in Jesus through the ministry of your church? If so, how does this impact the commitment to moving forward with a U-Turn vision?
- How would you describe the DNA of your church? What do you do naturally and consistently as a congregation? How does outreach fit into the normal flow of your church life?
- Share your story of how you came to faith in Jesus. Also share one

way you are experiencing God's presence and power in your life in recent days.

U-Turn Prayers

Gather with church friends, leaders, or small-group members and pray in the following directions:

- Pray that every believer in your church would see himself or herself as a person who bears and shares the light of Jesus on a daily basis.
- Ask God to help your church leaders make a personal commitment to include outreach as a normal part of their area of ministry.
- Thank God for the fruit He has grown and is bringing in through the ministry of your church.

11

The "Wow" Factor

by Bob Bouwer

What do visitors and guests say after coming to your church?
They should be saying, "Wow!"

One of my favorite words is *wow*. I have always liked it because I'm a very excitable person, and the word *wow* excites me. Whenever someone says, "Wow!" it means something exceptional has happened. "Wow, what a play!" "Wow, what a snowstorm!" *Wow* communicates that something outstanding has taken place.

God Desires the "Wow" Factor to Be Our Goal

The Bible does not use the word *wow*; however, the principle of *wow* is found throughout. In Genesis 1 and 2, God saw all that He had made and it was very good—Wow! All the places in Scripture that display the majesty and power of God are wows. Solomon's temple—talk about a Wow!

2 Chronicles 2:5: *"The temple I am going to build will be great, because our God is greater than all other gods."* And what a temple he built!

Jesus himself used the power of *wow*. He did miracles for three primary reasons. First, to prove that He was God and that He had power over illness, creation, and all things. Second, Jesus had a heart for those who were hurting, whether demonized, physically ill, or filled with sin. Third, He knew the miracles would draw a crowd, and when they came, He would call them to repentance and proclaim the good news of forgiveness and restoration. When the crowd witnessed a healing, they would go and tell others about Jesus. Mark 7:37 states this: *"People were overwhelmed with amazement. 'He has done everything well,' they said. 'He even makes the deaf hear and the mute speak.'"*

God was intentional in using the analogy of a bride when describing the Church. At a wedding, the bride and groom become one. We are one with Jesus as He takes up residence in us. Jesus is the head of the Church as the groom. The bride is beautiful and attractive. The bride is what the world sees. We, the Church, must reflect the beautiful bride of Christ.

Lukewarmness Is Never Intended

People are not attracted to churches that are mediocre and display no passion. In Revelation 3, Jesus rebukes the lukewarm church. He wishes they were hot or cold, but because they are lukewarm, He is about to spit them out of His mouth. How a church presents herself in her messages, programs, services, and ministry reflects the energy put into it. We are never called to mediocrity, offering a bare-minimum amount of energy to maintain a church. We're called to make the church attractive to people in every way we possibly can. We are called to be extreme. Many Christians, over time, lose the extreme passion they once had for Christ and subsequently their churches become mediocre, maintenance churches. God calls us to an extreme passion for Him and for the lost, and this is the attraction to those looking on from the outside.

People in new churches never start out lukewarm. They become lukewarm by virtue of various circumstances. When Faith Reformed Church was founded almost fifty years ago, the members were an extreme *hot*. They were filled with evangelistic fire. They were filled with a strong desire to reach people outside the kingdom of God and see God call and bring them in. And God did. They grew from a few members to many members. Those many members began a building project that soon became their church home. Gone were the folding chairs in the middle-school gym, and now came the wow of seeing God fill their new church. And fill it He did. There were plenty of wows to celebrate.

However, over the years, what began as a wow subtly become a *whoa*. Faith Church was a good church filled with godly born-again Christians. She had a great history of support for missions and a close sense of community, but admittedly things that at one time had been hot had become lukewarm.

In 1990, when I became a pastor on staff at Faith Church, part of my search team investigation revealed that something was wrong. We didn't use words like *wow* or *whoa* at the time, but we agreed that was our story.

A Survey of the Surrounding Towns

It wasn't until we did a survey in the community that God began revealing to me the power of wow. A few of us decided to survey a three-town radius to discover the perception of the local Protestant churches. It was indeed revealing. Among the 175 adults we talked to, we never met an atheist. In fact, everyone had some "religious background" but very few went to church. When asked why they didn't attend, the number one reason was boredom or irrelevancy.

Analyzing Why Church Is Considered Irrelevant

After gathering the results from the survey, we asked ourselves why people perceived the church as boring and irrelevant and how we could change their perception. A bit of American Protestant church history is necessary for us to understand what has happened in America. Almost all American Protestant churches can trace their roots to Western Europe: the Lutheran Church to Germany; the Reformed Church to the Netherlands; the Episcopal Church to England; the Presbyterian Church to Scotland; the Catholic Church to Italy; and the Covenant Church to Sweden. All this is to say that if you look at American Christian churches, they look like Western European churches transplanted onto new soil.

In my own denomination, the Reformed Church in America, our polity, our theology, our church buildings, our music, our dominant ethnicity can all be traced to the Netherlands. In this we find the problem. While America has developed its own culture, with its own dynamics unique to America, the church has remained very Western European in appearance and practice. The result is that our church worshiped like Europe in an American culture, resulting in a clash of cultures.

Take, for example, music. You can go up and down the AM/FM dial and you will no longer find pipe organ music. America is listening to pop, jazz, rock and roll, hip-hop, etc. If we are going to be culturally relevant, we have to understand what people consider to be exciting and relevant.

Even our buildings reveal our source. Most of the churches I grew up in looked like European buildings with stained glass, long and narrow structures, four or five stairs up to a platform with a choir loft behind it. Again, not wrong or bad, just very Western European.

The result is that churches have become irrelevant to the culture around them, for those within the church and for those outside. Many of those within have realized they are culturally irrelevant. We had to figure out how to return to a "wow" church before any kind of outreach efforts could be fruitful. If God could make our own people say, *Wow!* they would want others to experience a wow as well.

Becoming a Relevant "Wow" Church

People return to experience things they have determined are a wow. I once read that if a person goes to a restaurant that they rate a 5 on a 1 to 5 scale, they will tell ten to fifteen people about it in the next twenty-four hours. Right down the street from our church a new breakfast and lunch restaurant opened called the Scrambled Diner. The first time I went, I rated it a 5. The food was good, fresh, and healthy. The service was warm and friendly and the décor was pleasing to the eye. Since then, I have joked with the owner that I should get a commission because I have been there so often and told so many people about it. I recommend the restaurant because it is a wow.

We worship a "wow" God! Look at His creation each spring. Look at the mountains or deep into the sea and you will say, *Wow!* Unfortunately, that is not what people often say about churches. Again, I say the key to a U-Turn church is to ask God to make it a "wow" church.

"Wow" Worship

For Faith Church, we began with worship. We studied "wow" churches around the country for an entire year. We asked ourselves what made us say "Wow!" about them. We said it about their music, the arts, the messages, and the fellowship. We said it about the joy in worship and the focus and the theme of the day. We even said it about their use of technology.

Based on our year of study, we determined that the first U-Turn would have to take place in our adult worship. We prayed, studied, poured resources and staff into creating a new experience in worship that looked and felt American. For us, it meant changing the worship style from traditional Western European to a contemporary American style. We went from robed choirs to singers, ensembles, and a periodic gospel choir. We went from hymn books to songs with the words on screens.

Slowly but surely we began to hear people say, *Wow!* It meant our worship was a wonderful experience. Then we asked our people to invite their friends, family members, and co-workers to one of our services. We gave them ideas and tools, such as printed invitations to hand out.

Almost all of the guests that came would say, *Wow!* Sometimes it was "Wow, that's too loud!" But most of the time it was "Wow, the music was great!" or "Wow, the screens are cool!" or "Wow, that message was applicable to my life!" But most important, we told them about a God who loves them in a very powerful way through His Son Jesus Christ.

"Wow" Children's Ministry

After God transformed our worship from whoa to wow, we began to methodically evaluate all areas of ministry and ask God to change each ministry from whoa to wow.

A group of young moms came together before the consistory board. They presented a strategic plan to make a U-Turn in our children's ministry. They wanted to transform our Sunday school ministry into a "wow" children's ministry. The board unleashed them, and the rest is history.

It all began at a children's conference, where they were introduced to a new model of Sunday school: something relevant, safe, inviting, and yes, even fun. Research by the Barna Group was shared: "If you want to shape a person's life—whether you are most concerned about his or her moral, spiritual, physical, intellectual, emotional, or economic development—it is during these crucial eight years [five-to-twelve-year-old range] that lifelong habits, values, beliefs, and attitudes are formed."[1] They asked themselves how they could make the most of the opportunity before us to reach kids for Christ.

A team of five women met weekly to plan and pray. They were challenged by Sue Miller, the director of the children's ministry at Willow Creek Community Church, who said, "I'm reminded about the power unleashed by a team's willingness to change their ministry. Children need ministries BOLD enough to abandon the safety of 'the way we've always done it' in favor of programs that relevantly and creatively share the timeless truth of God's love and grace. We honor God when we decide to do whatever it takes to reach today's kids so that they know and love Jesus."[2] They understood that the message of the gospel does not change, but the method continues to change. The team approached me with this compelling vision. I, in turn, caught the vision and asked for the board's ear and subsequent buy-in. It was a risk, but they were willing to take it.

In November 1998, during our Sunday school hour, we ran a pilot program to raise enthusiasm and to give children, parents, and leaders a picture of what a new model of children's ministry could be. We could see God at work as children were lined up waiting to come into the gym. Security name tags were distributed (the #1 concern for new families is the safety of their children), and as the doors opened, new worship songs could be heard, and children raced to the crafts and games that were spread out across the gym. During the hour, children learned new songs, listened to a teaching by a gifted communicator, and then divided into small groups where leaders used activities to apply the lesson to the children's lives.

As a result, new children came to Treasureland. We heard stories of them urging their parents to come to church. Today, more than six hundred children below fifth grade are learning about Jesus in a relevant, safe, inviting, and fun way. *Wow!*

I had always dreamed of a church where my children would line up just as they would at an amusement park to get into the church and the children's ministry. After these women took the reins, I remember one moment when I said, *Wow!* I came around the corner toward our church gym, where the new experience called Treasureland was held. I saw two of my four children lined up about twenty-five children back, jumping up and down waiting for the gym doors to open. They were excited to experience a *wow* led by leaders in action-packed children's worship tailored for them. A dream come true!

"Wow" Greeting

Another area where we needed a U-Turn was in greeting people. The research on the importance of human touch was eye-opening. There have been numerous such studies with common results. Human touch is known to contribute to physical healing, career success, ability to love others, and even to increase honesty in people. On the flip side, the lack of human touch contributes to depression, isolation, feelings of unworthiness, and insecurity. Some people can go day after day and never receive a single touch from another human being. If you read anything about this subject, you'll find that a simple handshake or pat on the back has more impact on humans than most people think.

We realized that not only do people need and desire human touch from greeters, but greeters play a huge factor in people's first impressions. Within the first few minutes of being at an establishment, people will have formed an opinion of it and will have decided in their minds whether or not they would be willing to return. It takes at least three times the amount of time to change an opinion once it has been formed.

Faith Church implemented a Greeting Team with a three-touch rule. We placed greeters outside (sub-zero or 95 degrees plus), greeters inside the atrium, and greeters inside the worship center. Our goal was to have every individual welcomed with multiple touches and smiles before the service started. The individuals joining the Greeting Team have a heart for it. Our previous method was to ask each member to greet at an assigned service whether they wanted to or not.

Nine out of ten guests reported back that their first wow was being greeted. Today, we continue to receive positive feedback on the Greeting Team.

It sounds very biblical—*"Greet one another."*

"Wow" Aesthetics

Titus 2:10: *"So that in every way they will make the teaching about God our Savior attractive."* Paul is speaking here to the character of a slave, but surely in all things we should be seeking to "make the teaching about God our Savior attractive."

When we drive through a neighborhood and see a house in disrepair, perhaps the paint peeling, the fence missing slats, the bushes needing trimming, we think to ourselves, consciously or unconsciously, that a little TLC is needed. Yet in our churches, we sometimes make excuses for unappealing facilities, saying we're being good stewards of the Lord's money or that God cares about more important things than paint on the walls. God does care about the more important things, but the more important things are what drive us to care about the rest. God has gifted some with an eye for color and design and decoration to make a pleasing, warm, inviting environment for people. Wouldn't you think that God smiles, knowing His children are using the gifts He gave them, not just in their own homes, but first and foremost in the buildings where His children meet and worship Him? In the book of Haggai, God told the Israelites that they were to rebuild the temple. Yet the Israelites procrastinated. God approached them and said: *" 'Is it a time for you yourselves to be living in your paneled houses, while this house remains a ruin? . . . Go up into the mountains and bring down timber and build the house, so that I may take pleasure in it and be honored,' says the LORD."*[3]

The church is not just a building but God's believing people. However, we believe the church building where God's people worship should be attractive, pleasing, and welcoming to the world. I believe this is universally important. I've worshiped in the Philippines, the Dominican Republic, and China, and each place, in their own way, created a "wow" environment. The key is being able to live in the tension between focusing too much on the place and not caring at all. Many third-world countries are known to put more care into the aesthetics of their places of worship than in their own homes. We are not biblically required to decorate in a specific way as God instructed in the Old Testament. The freedom is ours to choose the color of the walls, the texture of the carpeting, and the style of the furniture. But the goal of making it a "wow" church should still be there. The physical building you are holding church services in, whether it is a high school gym or a Gothic cathedral, can be made attractive to the people you desire to reach.

We formed what we call the Design Team that enjoys visiting other churches and getting ideas. The team consists of both professional and nonprofessional decorators. They enjoy brainstorming, shopping, painting, creating, and making the church aesthetically wow.

"Wow" Communication

People will ask me what I would do differently if I had it to do over. My answer is that I would *communicate* more right from the start. Even when I thought I was communicating, it wasn't enough. At one point our staff was having a tough season; some people were feeling that they weren't being heard or they were uninformed about what was going on church-wide. We started what we called "staff infection." I know, it's a weird name (a staph infection in the medical field is a bacterial infection that is contagious). Our staff infection is a good thing; it's about spreading the news of what's happening. Our entire staff gathers every Wednesday morning for a half hour or more to be heard and to hear from others about what is going on.

Each department gives a recap of anything new. It has proven to be fun, informative, unifying, and most of all communicative.

If the staff was feeling out of the loop, we realized that communication to the congregation could also be improved. We offer a monthly newsletter called "In the Loop" so no individual feels "out of the loop." We have a Midweek Update e-newsletter that goes out to all members and regular attendees, updating them on what is currently going on in the church. We print announcements in the weekly church service bulletin. Occasionally, we have announcements from the pulpit. For a season at Faith Church, we had "The Announcement Guys." These two men would videotape themselves in a different location every week and share the announcements in a fun and comical way at the beginning of services. The creative settings would be chosen with the announcements in mind. For instance, the details announcing the half-marathon our church was involved in was filmed at a local school's running track.

In general, communication must be a wow. Whether the individual is a staff member or an attendee, good communication makes individuals feel they belong. It gives them ownership in their church because they are not left out of the loop.

Conclusion

We continue seeking to move from whoa to wow in every department. We do one area at a time, and sometimes we have to tell people, "Not yet." We have gone through the areas of adult worship, children's ministry, greeters, volunteers, theology, facilities, young adult ministries, and multi-sites. Currently we are working on youth and missions.

Are we a perfectly "wow" church? No. Are we hearing lots of wows? Yes. What's next? Pastoral care, training of leaders, and mini-churches (small groups).

After consulting churches and hosting conferences, I can say with confidence that the power of wow is key. It is so delightful for me to come to a church and say, "Wow, they are making some great U-Turns!" Ultimately, we can say, "Wow, what a God!"

"Whatever you do, do it all for the glory of God." [4] From the Treasureland

volunteers to the worship team; to the pastors delivering the messages to the clean-up crew; to the Security Team to the Design Team that keeps the building fresh and stylish; to the Flower Team that lines our walkways with beautiful plants and flowers, we do it all for the glory of God, giving it the best we possibly can—and you can too.

Kevin's Reflections on the "Wow" Factor

Corinth Church came at this topic from a different perspective. As a small church with a country feel, the idea of doing things that would wow visitors might not have connected for our people. With a hundred years of history, a rich Dutch heritage, and a high value for humility, this concept would have been a hard sell.

Instead of talking about creating "wow" ministries and experiences, we talked more about excellence. We would seek to do the best we could in every area of our ministry. This is a helpful distinction, because some leaders and churches that read this book might be in a community like Bryon Center, Michigan. Focusing on the "wow" factor might not make sense in your church setting. But you can get a lot of the same results if you call your church members and leaders to seek to do everything with excellence for the glory of God.

If you seek to do children's ministry with excellence so you can serve kids in the church and reach kids outside of the church, this might make sense for some people. If you seek excellence in how you greet and welcome people, this could make sense to your church members. If you strive for excellence in your music, nursery care, the condition of your building, small groups, and every other area of your ministry, this will help you move forward.

This might seem like a word game, but it is not. At Corinth Church, talking about trying to create "wow" experiences would not have resonated for many of our church members, and because of that fact it would not have moved us forward. But calling people to a new level of excellence brought about similar results and created a framework that made sense for our church.

If you took a tour of the facilities of Corinth Church and Faith Church, you would notice a number of differences. Both churches have purchased land and added significant physical space over the last decade. Faith has more of a "wow" feeling as you walk around. The adult Sunday school classes look like beautiful living rooms. There are large-screen TVs strategically positioned around the buildings. The coffee shop is warm and inviting. The bookstore is top-notch. It is a "wow" facility. The new space at Corinth is clean, well built, but has a simpler, more common feel. There is a sense of excellence, but honestly, it is not as impressive. A walk around Corinth's facility would not lead to declarations of *"Wow!"* But it is the right space and feel for this unique congregation.

One thing you will learn on your U-Turn journey is that there is not an absolute right and wrong way of doing things. The question is, what is right for your church? On this particular topic, Corinth and Faith took different routes, but both moved forward on the U-Turn adventure.

U-Turn Exercises and Activities

U-Turn Exercises

1. List the areas in your church that you would say are a wow.
2. List the areas in your church that you would say are more in the "whoa" category.
3. Plan ways you can work together to improve the areas that need improvement.

U-Turn Leaders/Pastors Questions

1. What is the first area in your church that needs a U-Turn?
2. How would your guests or visitors internally rate your church upon their first experience?

WHOA |————————————————————| WOW

     1   2   3   4   5

The Never-Ending Journey of a U-Turn Church

"Are we there yet?"

"How much longer until we arrive?"

"Can we stop now?"

We have all been on family trips and heard comments like these. Parents try to calm the mounting storm in the backseat by assuring the restless passengers that "We will be there soon," "Just a few more minutes," or "Take a nap and we'll magically arrive by the time you wake up."

Sometimes on the U-Turn journey, we hear these exact same questions:

"Are we there yet?"

"How much longer until we arrive?"

"Can we stop now?"

The dilemma is, the U-Turn journey does not have a finish line . . . on this earth. A U-Turn is really a series of movements that recalibrate the focus and direction of the church toward the heart and the will of God. We need to make these turns over and over and over again.

Both Faith Church and Corinth have been in the U-Turn process for almost two decades, and there is a sense that we are just getting started.

What do we do when the road seems long and voices are crying out, "Are we there yet?"

- *Remember, Jesus is with us on the journey.* He is both a travel partner and our final destination.
- *Hold heaven in your hearts.* When we reach our final destination (and every follower of Jesus will), the bumps in the road we experienced on earth will not begin to compare to the glory of being forever with our Savior.
- *Keep inviting more people to join you on the journey.* As long as we have breath and life, we can keep reaching out.
- *Refuse to listen to the lies and myths.* We can't grow discouraged and give up . . . what we are doing is too important.
- *Make it personal.* As we engage in a church-wide U-Turn, we can commit to always making a personal You-Turn. The only way the whole church will move forward is when individuals are following the heart and will of God.

Keep pressing on! God is at work in your life and church, and it will all be worth it when you hear the words, *"Well done, good and faithful servant!"* (Matthew 25:21).

12

U-Turn Myths

by Bob Bouwer

Addressing the myths in ministry can move your church
from maintenance to mission.

An elder once called me and asked me to meet him for lunch. I honestly didn't know why he wanted to meet with me, but I had a hunch that he wanted to address some of his concerns and fears about the church. When we sat down, he reached into his pocket and pulled out a list with about ten items that he wanted to discuss. He had heard about stereotypes of other churches and possible negative effects from the changes we were making. He became fearful because he treated these myths as truths. Once we walked through the items and talked about them, he gained his confidence back.

A myth is called a *myth* because it has not been proven true. People hear myths and allow them to impact their behavior as if they were true. They believe what is plausible rather than what is demonstratively true.

It was a very revealing moment for me to realize that a church could actually stop moving forward because of the fear of myths. In this chapter,

I am going to address each myth, exposing it and discussing the untruth in it.

Myth #1: The church will be ten miles wide and one inch deep.

This myth gives a false impression that the size of a church is directly correlated to the depth of its ministry. It implies that a large church will have to compromise its biblical and theological depth. This myth implies that if you desire a U-Turn, you're going to have to water down the gospel; you'll have to weaken your theological underpinnings.

A church that is one inch deep has deeper issues than size. The size of a church does not determine its depth. They are independent characteristics. Preaching and teaching the Word of God does not have to be compromised.

I believe that a church that desires to turn around will actually experience a deepening of their theological, biblical, and personal roots. Faith Church was intentional in making sure this myth would not be true for them.

Years ago, I was astonished to find out that many of the longtime members of the church were not reading their Bibles. I challenged them to read Scripture together and created a Bible-reading schedule. This schedule is a four-year reading plan, taking one chapter a day for six days a week, Monday through Saturday, leaving Sunday to read the passage from the message. I passed out the schedule to a few people and received so much positive feedback that I shared it with the entire church. As of this writing, we have more than two thousand people reading through the schedule. We have read through the entire Bible twice and are currently in our third time around. We also offer a daily meditation e-subscription called Daily Med. Every day someone can receive, through their e-mail or smart phone, a verse from the chapter for the day followed by a short meditation, available to those outside of our church as well.[1] Many share their testimonies of how reading the Bible every day has changed their lives and how amazing it is that a little check box is all they needed for the accountability to keep reading.

We also offer a variety of classes, which include the following topics: Reformed theology, how to read the Bible, God as our Father, discovering your spiritual gifts, specific books of the Bible, and many others. Through these classes, we provide opportunity for spiritual growth.

How do you know if this is truly a myth in your church? The only way to really tell is to listen to the people in the church and listen to the feedback from visitors. Visitors often come up to me after a service telling me how much they enjoyed it and how glad they are that I preach from the Bible. It always makes me smile because I'm thinking *of course,* but realize that this myth gives visitors the preconceived notion that preaching from the Bible is rare in a large church. Our people know that Faith Church is Reformed in its theology and solid in its evangelical belief of the authority of Scripture. The Bible tells us: *"Watch your life and doctrine closely."*[2] We take that command seriously. We have proven this myth untrue, and your church can too.

Myth #2: It's only about entertainment.

In our case, we made the shift from a traditional style of worship to a more contemporary style. As soon as we made that shift, people started saying that Faith Church was growing only because it was entertaining and adapting church to a Hollywood style.

I can understand why they would say that, because in a traditional church you might not use video, drums, or guitars. An element had changed. The root of the issue had nothing to do with entertainment, but understanding the culture.

By definition, entertainment is something engaging. All worship should be to the glory of God, using music, prayers, Scripture, and fellowship to engage people with God and with each other. God created this world for us to enjoy. Worship should be enjoyable and worship should be engaging. Worship involves our minds, bodies, and emotions. God made us with the ability to smile, cry, and express other emotions that are incorporated into worship to allow us to be passionate, concerned, challenged, and engaged.

Studying the tabernacle worship in an Old Testament class in seminary, I learned how joyful, engaging, and exuberant worship was for the people. All along the path from Bethlehem to Jerusalem, the families and community would walk together, chanting and singing the psalms in preparation for worshiping in the temple. In the same way, Christ provides us the place of worship as we gather together in the name of Christ to engage in worshiping Him. Worship should be nothing less than joyful, engaging, and exciting. It is an experience that creates the desire to invite others so they can experience worshiping Christ too.

If you are a fan of a particular ball club and your team is having a good year, it's entertaining. Tickets are hard to come by and people want to be where the excitement is. Imagine how God would be glorified by a church so engaging that people would excitedly tell their friends about it!

I think the church has always known this. In a sense, the church has always been engaging. Huge choirs in matching robes singing cantatas are very engaging and have been in the church for hundreds of years. Special music during the offertory with the organist belting out her best rendition is very engaging. We are drawn toward God, in awe of the God-given gifts that are being offered in praise to Him. The changes that are being made are in style and instruments, not in purpose. Is it only about entertainment? We don't think so. It's about engaging people in worship, turning their focus on Jesus Christ.

Myth #3: All the people will leave and the church will fall apart.

The third myth is that if we make the changes to turn around, people will leave and the church will fall apart. The truth is that you *may* lose some people. Yes, we lost some people in our U-Turn experience, but the vast majority of people stayed.

One of the fears people had was that older members would leave, and our church would consist only of young people. At Faith Church, the elderly stayed. Those that left were from the mid-generation, ages fifty-five to sixty-five. I believe this was because they were the ones who worked at building the church and felt betrayed when changes were being made. I think one of the reasons the elderly stayed is because they saw their grandchildren coming alive in Christ. It's possible too that the elderly are that much closer to heaven and realize there are more important issues to worry about than the style of music in a church. Whatever the reason, the fact is that about sixty-five people left, but the majority of our number stayed and many others joined. At any given point in the U-Turn process, we always had more members than before the U-Turn began.

Following is a testimony from an elder in our church, a charter member, who was not happy with all the changes that were being made.

My Personal U-Turn
by Elmer VanDrunen

As a part of the church's leadership, I was on board and happy with the decision to become a church that was reaching out to "religiously disconnected people." Though not defined in those exact terms, this was the church's heart from its earliest days. However, we weren't too far into the process when I developed some misgivings about changes we were making. The situation became especially acute to me when the decision was made to be singularly focused, meaning that traditional style worship services were eliminated. Instead of singing hymns rich in theology and memories, we sang praise songs that were unfamiliar and, to me, "unsingable." With the other changes taking place it seemed it wasn't "my church" any longer, and as someone who was there when the church started, it didn't seem fair.

Others were feeling the same way, many of them fellow charter members. Some of them appealed to me to do something since I was in a leadership position. I know there were those who felt that I had forsaken my theological moorings. It was especially painful to watch very good friends, fellow charter members, leave and find new church homes. I am sure some of them felt betrayed. Although we are still friends with many of them, we don't have the closeness we once had.

I knew our children and grandchildren, who were a part of the church, were enthused with the changes that were being made. Church to them was never better!

I rejoiced in the "fruit" that the church experienced. There was a new enthusiasm by many. There were many new faces, and the greatest thing was the number of people experiencing life change. However, I wasn't sure I could handle these changes for the rest of my life. I pondered whether I would leave or stay.

One day, while weighing my options, my thoughts turned to the appreciation I have for cross-cultural missionaries. For many years, I have looked on them as world-class heroes. I reflected on the price they pay and the sacrifices they make in order that Christ's name can be known and that He can be worshiped in a strange, difficult, and sometimes dangerous place. At some point in this solitary discourse, God spoke to my heart and asked a very simple question, "Elmer, why can't you be a missionary in your own church?"

A positive answer to that question has given me a whole new perspective. I don't have to appreciate every aspect of the worship services. I don't have to like every change that has been made. Even if it doesn't feel like "my church," I am reminded that it never *was* "my church." It has been His all along.[5]

Elmer's assessment is correct. It isn't the pastor's church; it isn't the charter member's church; it is God's church. If you can understand that you're part of a mission and you're becoming outreach-driven, seeking those who are far from God, you will begin to see yourself as missionaries going into their culture.

Myth #4: Make changes and the money will stop.

The next myth is that if we make changes, people will stop giving. A few years into the process of our U-Turn, I was stopped by a man who said, "You know, Bob, if you keep these changes up you're going to feel it in the wallet, because I know a lot of people who have lots of money will leave the church." The Lord doesn't need any one particular person's money. In Faith Church's story, when we needed money in order to continue, the money was there. The myth simply is not true.

I'll admit that I was always afraid of losing money. I was afraid too of taking a risk, but I have learned from our experiences. Leaders in the church kept encouraging me, saying, "Bob, there's a lot more money out there than you think." Trusted leaders from other churches encouraged me and said, "If God could create a vision and a mission in your church, there will never be a money issue." And that's our story. Year after year, there wasn't a single time when we didn't have the needed financial resources.

There were times when we increased our budget from one year to the next by 50 percent, and I remember thinking this was crazy. But at the end of the year we would always make our budget. Even in 2009, when America was in the midst of recession, we came through April, and paused. At the pace we were going, compared to other years, the projected outcome looked as if we would end up a million dollars behind budget. We made some adjustments, and we tightened our belt. As the year went on, we started to see people rise to the occasion, and we ended the year ahead of budget. This doesn't say so much about who we are but about who God is and that He is in control.

A long time ago, a church in our community developed a relationship with Faith Church. One of the leaders of that church would meet with me once in awhile for coffee. A statement he shared that has always stayed with me was that "talent begets talent and God's blessing brings God's blessings." I have experienced this to be true. When God is behind something, He will take very little and produce a lot. The stories in the Bible, such as the parable of the widow's mite, the increase of the loaves and fish, and Gideon and his dwindling army, teach us what God can do. I absolutely believe that when God is honored, when God is sought, when the vision is from the Lord, God blesses it. God has proved faithful to us at Faith Church. God is drawing thousands of people to himself and is providing resources we never imagined.

Myth #5: We can't do it.

The next myth is that "We can't do it." We host U-Turn church conferences, inviting churches from many areas. Pastors, elders, deacons, leaders, and staff members coming from rural, suburban, and city churches will hear our U-Turn principles. We have often seen the "we can't do it" attitude. They will say that they're not Corinth Church or Faith Church, and I understand that.

The "we can't do it" myth has some truth to it, because it is true that *we* can't do it, but *God* can, and with His help *we* can. Every church has potential, and a U-Turn can be accomplished with God's help. It doesn't have to be done the exact same way as another church, and it won't be, but it can be done. It is possible that a rural church can turn around. It is possible that a church with a 300-year history can turn around. It's possible that a young urban church can turn around. All things are possible with God.

God often uses *"the foolish things of the world to shame the wise . . . the weak things of the world to shame the strong."* [6] Back in the mid-'90s, during some of the really difficult times, the song "He Is Able," by Rory Noland and Greg Ferguson, ministered to me. It's a simple song that we used in services, and it quickly became known as my favorite song. There was a lot of teasing about playing "Bob's favorite song" *again*. I probably did overuse the song. But during that season of my ministry, those words infused vitality and strength when I needed it the most. It reminded me of the fact that God is able to do immeasurably more than we could ever ask or imagine.

My hope for Faith Church is that we will always believe that God is able, that He can do what seems impossible to us. That's my hope for you; that's my hope for every church of Jesus Christ around the world. *God is able.*

Myth #6: I need to know everyone.

The "I need to know everyone" myth is definitely 100 percent false. The comfort zone of familiarity is nice. However, the truth is that you do not need to know everyone in your church. Once it gets beyond a certain size, whether it's 400 or 4,000, it's impossible to know everyone. You need to know the One who does know everyone in your church. Jesus is the common bond. Outreach cannot be compromised because a church doesn't want to stretch its comfort zone.

The solution is the mini-church model. Some churches call them small groups or cell groups, but the idea is the same. You don't have to know everyone in your church, but you can know everyone in your mini-church. Members must intentionally join a small group of people that gather with the common goal of growing spiritually and walking alongside each other. This topic could be a book in itself, but my point is simply that a large church must encourage mini-churches to avoid the isolation myth.

Myth #7: The pastor will stand alone.

The lonely pastor myth implies that the pastor will be the target of all the negativity and will stand alone. It implies that the pastor and his family must bear the load alone because that is their job.

During our U-Turn process, I awoke one night with an extreme attack of anxiety. I felt that I might have messed up authorizing all the changes we were making. I felt all alone, and my wife shared that she felt the same way. We had been receiving a lot of criticism from a vocal minority of people, but the majority was silent. We thought the majority supported us, but we weren't hearing from them and we felt alone.

That Sunday night we went to our mini-church gathering. One of the members of our group could see the anxiety on my face and asked if we were okay. My wife began to cry. Then I began to cry. I expressed how alone we felt and how scared we were. What they said next was a defining moment for us. They responded by saying that if the only ones left in Faith Church were the eight of us, we would still be a church. They declared that they loved us and stood behind us 100 percent, no matter what happened. That encouragement gave us confidence and our joy back. I cannot stress enough how important that night was to us.

Pastors, find a support group. If you are not in a mini-church, form a group with people that will walk with you. You are not alone. The myth is false. In turn, encourage your leaders and support their decisions.

Members and layleaders, encourage your pastor. If you support your pastor, let him know it. Do not remain silent. The U-Turn process requires encouragement and support from one another.

What are the myths that have tripped you up? Is there a myth your church is believing that prevents you from moving forward? Look at the myths listed in this chapter and determine for yourself whether or not they are true. And remember, with God's help, anything is possible.

Kevin's Reflections on U-Turn Myths

In this chapter, Bob looked at seven common myths that often surface when a church begins to make a U-Turn. Faith Church faced all of these and so did Corinth, to varying degrees. I would like to look briefly at two additional myths Corinth Church ran into along the way.

Myth #8: We will have to compromise on God's Word and our doctrines.

This was a huge fear for long-term church members who had a deep love for the Scriptures and Reformed theology. They were afraid we were trying to become a mega-church with watered down beliefs and convictions. As you move forward in your commitment to make a U-Turn, get ready for people to express fear that compromise is on the horizon.

We battled this myth in two very specific ways. First, we preached God's Word with clarity and passion. No compromise. Second, we made sure our children's ministry, youth ministry, men's and women's ministries, and every other ministry was built on the solid rock of Scripture and sound doctrine.

It did not take long for people to see that we could be a growing and outreach-oriented church and still hold securely to the teaching of Scripture and our doctrines. As a matter of fact, both Faith Church and Corinth Church are known to be fairly conservative in theology and unapologetic about our commitment to God's Word and the truth it reveals.

Myth #9: Big churches are cold and impersonal.

As the church began to grow, this myth became almost a knee-jerk response of fear in the hearts of many longtime members and attendees: "Corinth will lose its warmth and friendly feeling." "What if we become an impersonal church that doesn't really care about people?"

We began to speak the truth to those who were being influenced by this myth. We let people know that a small church can be warm and welcoming, or it can be cold and unwelcoming. And a large and growing church can be very impersonal, or extremely friendly and personal. The issue is not size, but a choice to value people and connect them to each other.

Although Corinth Church and Faith Church have grown larger and larger over the years, they remain two of the most friendly and embracing congregations I have ever seen. When I talk to those who visit Corinth for the first time, they almost all make a comment about how the people reached out to them and extended kindness. I hear the same from those who come to Faith Church as visitors. Both Faith and Corinth are great examples of how a growing church can become more personal if we make a commitment to reach out and create structures to connect people to each other.

U-Turn Exercises and Activities

U-Turn Reflection Questions

1. Of the myths listed in this chapter, which ones cause the most concern for you?

2. Is there a myth or myths that your church believes now?

3. What will you and your staff do to change this thinking and defuse these myths?

U-Turn Exercises

If there are myths that still plague your congregation, plan a series of messages or workshops where these misbeliefs can be addressed and dealt with.

U-Turn Prayer

Heavenly Father, show us what myths we are tempted to believe or are struggling with, and help us to address them and dispel them in our midst so that we are all on the same page, seeking your will for our church and following the instruction of your Word in all the ministries we are involved in. Glorify your name in our church body, and extend your kingdom through us. In Jesus' name we pray. Amen.

13

You-Turns:
From You-Turn to U-Turn

by Bob Bouwer

You-Turns Begin in Individual Hearts

Because we believe that the speed of the leader becomes the speed of the team, and eventually of the congregation, it is important for the "You-Turn" to begin with the pastor. Too often the church desires to turn around, but the leader's or leaders' internal lives are not prepared for what lies ahead. We have hosted at least ten U-Turn conferences, and each time we have watched God do some amazing You-Turns during the closing worship session. After the meditation, I invite participants to come to the front of the auditorium if they are in need of a personal You-Turn.

We explain that they may need this turnaround because they are burned out, worn out, over-tired, exhausted, or simply have no energy. They may come forward to surrender their life again because they've been living a lie. Or they are proclaiming and professing with their lips what has no basis in their hearts. Perhaps it is simply a matter of dwindling faith. Or it could be something far more serious: sexual sin, substance abuse, and the list goes on. The point is, in order for God to use them in leading their church in a U-Turn, they have to experience a You-Turn themselves.

It always fascinates me what God does during these times. We pray as they come forward, and when we open our eyes, the front of the auditorium is teeming with people on their knees before the Lord.

I've often been brought to tears by hearing the stories of what God does and is doing in these individuals. One pastor came forward and confessed to me that he was an alcoholic and his wife wasn't aware of his struggle. At the opposite end of the platform, a woman was praying with an elder of our church. She said her husband was an alcoholic and he didn't know it. At some point we realized these two were married! Six months later we received a letter from this pastor and his wife, celebrating what God had done. He is involved in a Celebrate Recovery Program and his marriage and his ministry are more solid than ever before. His change has preceded the U-Turn in their church.

The most common pastoral issue has to do with brokenness. Pastors have been leading churches and trying hard to do the things that would bring people to Christ. They have been trying to get those in their churches fired up, and they become discouraged by the results. To see how God refills them, inspires them, motivates them, and renews them by His Spirit and His Word is something to behold.

You-Turns in the Bible

Of course, the Bible is full of stories of individuals who experienced You-Turns, and the changes in their lives were significant.

David was a man after God's own heart, but there were some very dark times in his life, particularly when he fell into sin with Bathsheba and then arranged for the murder of her husband, Uriah. The Psalms reveal David's strong remorse and repentance. The Lord restored him and reignited him.

God's plan for Jonah was to use him to turn around the people of Nineveh, but Jonah ran from the plan. We all know that Jonah's You-Turn began in the belly of a fish.

And then there was Saul, who thought he was serving God by

persecuting and even killing Christians to slow down the church. The Lord turned him around on the road to Damascus and gave him a new name.

A You-Turn is what redemption is all about. God turns people toward himself, away from the path of sin and onto the path that He has planned for them.

You-Turn Moments

As I mentioned before, there is great power in decision. You can discuss something at length, and even be in agreement about it, and still not take any action. I ask pastors, "Do you create moments where people can make the decisions necessary to turn around?"

Testimonies of God's work in people's lives serve as powerful instruments of encouragement and motivation for others. During a series of messages on forgiveness, we placed an actual working door on the platform and invited people to physically walk through the "door of forgiveness."

Periodically we ask people to share testimonies of their journey through addiction, abuse, or other struggles. Afterward, I suggest to the congregation that perhaps this is *your* story, encouraging others to identify with a particular sin or failure so they can seek God's help as well. We must create opportunities for people to make a decision about how they will turn their lives around with God's help.

Another way to do this is to give an altar call, where people have the opportunity to come forward and kneel before God, confessing their sins quietly, or asking for prayer and counsel as needed. We have also had people write on a piece of paper, stating that today they are putting an end to a particular sin or behavior and turning their life back over to the Lord. Then they sign it as a final affirmation. The paper could be torn to pieces as a symbolic act of repentance and commitment, or pinned to a cross at the front of the sanctuary. Sometimes keeping the paper serves as a reminder to some.

Be creative about making opportunities for people to decide to make a You-Turn.

The Power of You-Turn Church Testimonies

You-Turn stories become contagious. Everyone has a story. Everyone needs to make a You-Turn. Not just when they come to Christ, but whenever they are drawn away from the Lord or His purposes for their life. I received the testimony below from a member of our congregation who is now on staff in full-time ministry:

> Dear Bob,
>
> I just wanted to take a moment while it's on my mind to say "thank you." I'll briefly explain. The other day I was watching my son at baseball practice. I was in my car because it was drizzling a bit. I reached under my seat for my Bible, turned off the radio, and turned to the book of John. I was so taken with the passage that I went home after the practice and broke out a commentary and dove in some more. About twenty minutes in, I stopped and asked myself, "What am I doing? Why don't I have the TV on? If somebody sees me, they'll laugh." Then it hit me how different I am, and it made me grin.
>
> I remember years ago when you challenged me to read the Bible. You said you would do it with me, one chapter a day. I remember at first saying no because I thought the Bible was boring. You kept after me and I finally gave in. I distinctly remember going through the book of Genesis. All those stories that I learned as a kid in Sunday school came back. But something was vastly different. Something inside of me was stirring. The best way to describe it is this: All that head knowledge, all that Jesus stuff, started to make its way from my head to my heart. I can honestly say I fell in love with the person, the real person, my best friend, Jesus Christ.
>
> Thanks for hanging in with me. Thanks for not giving up.[1]
>
> Yours in our best friend,
> Scott

There is power in testimony. It makes people think that if that person could do it, they could too.

When I was a young boy, in the mid '60s, early '70s, our church experienced what was known as the Lay Witness Movement. Laypeople from Chicago came up to our church in Wisconsin for a Sunday night service. They took over the meeting. It was the first time I had ever heard the term *laypeople* as a young boy. My thought was *What does* laypeople *mean? Do these people just lay around?* I asked my dad what the Lay Witness Movement meant. He told me it meant ordinary Christian people giving witness or testimony. The service was powerful. I remember it clearly still today. Ordinary Christians told stories of repentance from sin and about what God had done for them. They basically shared their You-Turn story. I remember their calling people in my church to come forward to repent and come back to the Lord. Watching that happen and seeing the life in our church as a result was fascinating to my young mind.

This happens today at our junior high retreats, senior high retreats, college-age retreats, adult retreats, marriage seminars, women's retreats, and men's retreats. These are the moments when God replenishes, restores, and reignites our lives. I call them You-Turns.

When was the last time you had a You-Turn experience? When has your church given opportunity for shared testimonies? These are defining moments that prepare a church for the U-Turn process.

We can think that our church is fine just the way it is. If we do things the way we have always done and there are no complaints, we may think we're on the right path, but we forget that the church is fallible. Of course, our head, Jesus Christ, is infallible, but the body, His Church, is in constant need of revival and renewal. We need the purifying fire of the Spirit. Church history shows us it's all about You-Turns.

You-Turn Movement

Churches that promote and experience You-Turns become attractive, inviting, and contagious. It may be counterintuitive, but it's true. When people hear other people's stories of turnarounds, no matter how spectacular or ordinary, they are encouraged and attracted to that kind of honesty.

We have heard from many of our current members that they kept coming back to our church because of the authenticity they saw here. One couple shared that they grew up in the church but quit going because they felt it was boring. Friends of theirs invited them to their church, but it was basically the same service they remembered from their youth. Everything was perfect and in order. They stood up at exactly the right spot, they sang the exact same words, methodically prayed, heard Scripture read, and listened to a message. They told their friends they didn't like their church. So the friends encouraged them to go to Faith Church, even though they didn't go there themselves. The couple came to Faith Church, heard the testimonies, and shared how everything seemed so real. When their friends who'd directed them here saw how alive in Christ they had become, they joined Faith Church too.

Our U-Turn story includes telling stories. We tell the big stories and the not-so-big stories. An elder tells a story, a widow tells a story, a twenty-something tells a story. We make opportunities to make known the work of God. The psalmist says, *"Make known among the nations what he has done."* [2] The church is the testimony of Christ to be seen *and* told.

When we were barely into the U-Turn process, a new believer shared her testimony on Christmas morning. I have asked her to share it in writing below:

Dear Faith Church,

My mom and dad were divorced when I was five. My dad was an alcoholic. By the time I was seven, I was molested. As a child, I weighed over 300 pounds. I remember praying to God, as a child, but somewhere along the line, I quit praying.

Five days before my eighteenth birthday, I was raped. I thought I'd lost it, and figured I'd be put in a rubber room.

I married at twenty-one, caught my husband with my best friend, and divorced at twenty-three. On a retaliation one-night stand with a man that I knew was a drunk, I became pregnant. I did not hide the fact that I was going to get an abortion. Nobody told me that it was wrong. But when I saw the fetus in a jar, a voice inside me told me that what I had done was wrong.

Soon after that, my brother passed away at the age of twenty-five.

At twenty-nine, I fell in love with a man and became pregnant. He was seeing another woman, and I ended the relationship. I chose to go against his wishes to have an abortion because I remembered that voice that spoke to me in the room where I'd had an abortion. I parented my beautiful daughter alone.

A woman at Faith Church offered to take my daughter, now about six years old, to church. For me, this was free babysitting so I always agreed. I was invited to see a play that my daughter was in at Faith Church, called "Zero to Hero." God used that children's play to change my life forever.

I watched the children share the message that God can take somebody who is a zero and make them a hero. The parents of the children were called to come up on stage, and I was horrified. Standing on that stage with the self-consciousness of being hundreds of pounds overweight made me feel that I was truly a zero. As I thought about how I viewed myself, the love of God poured into me the message of the play that I could go from a zero to a hero.

That night at home, I accepted Jesus into my life, and have been changed for all eternity. I cannot even describe the joy that I have now. I don't deserve it. None of us do. I had a hellish life and now I have Him. He is enough.

In a sense, the other areas in my life haven't changed much. I'm still a single mom. I still live on a poverty-level income, yet I know that He is more than enough! Why we go kicking and screaming along the way, I'll never know, because He is so good. He took me out of bondage, and I cannot describe the freedom I feel.

Shortly after I turned my life over to Jesus, I recall a moment when I was spending time alone with God and He whispered to my soul, "I was with you," and I pictured myself when I was that little girl sitting on my porch praying to God. Even though I felt alone, God was with me all along. He was with me then, He is with me now, and I know He will be with me in the future. That is my testimony to God's glory for all He has done for me![3]

Thank you.

Jen

Sharing personal information like this was new to Faith Church, and it had an especially powerful impact on Christmas morning. It was refreshing. I shared with the congregation that they may not have had the experiences that Jen had, but they could turn to Jesus for forgiveness and healing too. That Christmas morning, you could hear a pin drop in the sanctuary. The reality of the power of God had hit home.

Since that testimony many years ago, this woman has started a Bible study/support group ministry called First Place 4 Health to address the root issues behind overeating. She has lost 135 pounds, yet she will say that she has lost a lot more than that because she lost a lot of heavy baggage. Things will still get her down, but she knows the One who will carry her load for her. She has fully surrendered her life to Christ and is reaping the abundant life because of it.

When the unchurched, the de-churched, the irreligious, the lost, the neighbors, the seeking come to church for the first time and hear the You-Turn stories, it makes them feel safe. It's a place where they can become authentic. It's a place where they can feel comfortable telling *their* stories. Testimonies give hope. People don't feel alone anymore. Testimonies tell them that if God can bring those people out of their pit, God can turn their life around too. They are drawn to the authenticity. Testimonies are refreshing because society teaches us that our goal must be perfection, and we must pretend when things are not perfect. People also love to hear about God in action.

During a service in which we were covering the series we called Everyday Heroes, one of our pastors told his story about growing up in a home with mental illness. When he was eleven years old, his mom was diagnosed with schizophrenia and was in and out of mental hospitals the remainder of her life. From that time on, there was a sense of loss that he carried with him. Several years later in a time of prayer, our pastor asked God why he had to suffer life as he did when he was a child, and God met him. He experienced compassion and love from his heavenly Father. Scripture also portrays God as having some motherly traits, and this pastor received the motherly love that he craved. God was a mother to him in his time of need, and God also reminded him that He had provided surrogate mothers who had nurtured him along the way. God didn't instantly change his circumstances, but God changed him. After the service, many people came up to him, thanking him for sharing his story because they had a similar story. Some felt comforted that they were not alone in their suffering. Some shared that they were right in the middle of it, going through a similar experience with their own mother, and they had received hope through his testimony. It is important that we tell what the Lord has done in our lives.

You-Turn Mentality

We've all experienced it. You're going somewhere, you turn down the wrong street and instantly realize that you've made a wrong turn. You quickly turn around and get back on track. You may have also experienced this when you were on a trip and were not paying attention. You ended up taking the wrong highway, and before you knew it, you were an hour into the wrong direction. Similarly, our spiritual journey has You-Turn moments all along the way. Whether you've been on the wrong road a long time, just made a wrong turn, or are heading in the wrong direction, you need to turn around.

A You-Turn attitude in the church will continually remind people that transformation in Christ Jesus is and should be a reality for every Christian. Our journey contains many You-Turns because no one is perfect. Christ Jesus, through His Spirit, is on the journey with us, leading the way and telling us when we've made a wrong turn. Churches must be intentional about having a You-Turn mentality if they truly desire a U-Turn church. Faith Church would not be the church it is today if it were not for the many individuals who have experienced their own You-Turns.

God's desire is that you turn toward Him in all areas of your life and experience the plans He has for you.

God's desire for your church is that it turns toward Him and experiences the plans He has for it.

God desires that the changes in you and your church will reach others, even to the ends of the earth.

All it takes is one person who is willing to be authentic and share what God has done for them to begin a movement of You-Turns. An entire church can turn around, and it can begin with you.

U-Turn (You-Turn) Exercises and Activities

You-Turn Reflection Question

1. If you were at one of our conferences, and I invited you to come up and "You-Turn" your life during the closing worship, what would be the reason you'd come forward? What do you have to turn from? What is your story?

You-Turn Exercises

1. For yourself:
   a. I challenge you to put down this book right now, kneel before the Lord, tell Him you need a You-Turn, and become very specific about it.
   b. I urge you to tell two or three people who are close to you, in the next twenty-four hours, what God has done in you.
   c. Invite a friend to hold you accountable to the commitment you have made, once a week, via e-mail, text, or phone message.

2. For your church:

   Have your church leaders prepare a three-week series on the You-Turn experience of individuals. At the close of that three-week series, have a time at the end of your service where people can come forward to repent and pray for the Holy Spirit's help.

You-Turn Prayer

Heavenly Father, you know all things, and you know us better than we know ourselves. You know what's holding each one of us back from our full potential, even if we are not aware of it ourselves. Lord, we ask that you would turn us around and forgive us for our sins. Holy Spirit, make it very clear to us what it is that is holding us back from our own You-Turn. Help our church become a place that is inviting and attractive to others, a place that tells the story of what you have done in us.

Lord, turn us toward you and turn our church around for your glory. In Jesus' name. Amen.

Notes

Introduction: *Welcome to the Journey*

1. Schaeffer Institute Web site, "Statistics and Reasons for Church Decline," by Dr. Richard J. Krejcir, (*www.intothyword.org/articles_view.asp?articleid =36557&columnid=*).
2. Faith Church Web site: *www.faithchurchonline.org/*.
3. U-Turn information: *http://uturnministries.typepad.com/*.
4. Corinth Church Web site: *www.corinthreformed.org/index.cfm*.
5. Wayfarer Church Web site: *www.wayfarercc.org*.
6. In particular, both Bob and Kevin were influenced by the Willow Creek Conferences as well as the Saddleback Conferences.
7. RCA Web site: *www.rca.org/Page.aspx?pid=2225*.
8. Communicate on: *http://uturnministries.typepad.com/*.

Chapter 1: *Holy Zeal*

1. Revelation 2:4
2. Revelation 21:9
3. Ephesians 4:13
4. Luke 8:1–15
5. 1 Corinthians 3:6
6. Luke 15:1–7

Chapter 2: *Urgency*

1. Rick Warren was referring to Acts 2:41.
2. Bill Hull, *7 Steps to Transform Your Church* (Grand Rapids, MI: Baker Publishing Group, 1997), 11.
3. Revelation 22:17

4. Revelation 22:20

Chapter 4: *The Power of Prayer*
1. Bill Hybels, *Too Busy Not to Pray* (Westmont, IL: InterVarsity Press, 1988), 11.
2. 2 Corinthians 2:15
3. Matthew 21:13
4. Matthew 7:11
5. James 4:2
6. Mark 9:29
7. John Calvin, *Geneva Catechism*, 1542.
8. Hebrews 12:1

Chapter 5: *Biblical Truths vs. Personal Preferences*
1. James 1:17
2. Psalm 9:11
3. Psalm 92:1
4. Psalm 95:2
5. Psalm 40:3
6. Psalm 33:3; 96:1; 98:1; 149:1; Isaiah 42:10

Chapter 6: *Unleashing Leaders*
1. 1 Peter 2:4–10; Revelation 1:6; 5:10
2. There are a number of great resources you can find online if you search for: Bruce Bugbee Books: *What You Do Best in the Body of Christ; Discover Your Spiritual Gifts the Network Way.* I would also recommend the whole *Leadershift* program by Don Cousins.
3. Matthew 26:14–16
4. 1 Corinthians 12; Romans 12; Ephesians 4
5. See note 2.
6. If you search on Zondervan's Web site and look for Network, you can find the newest versions of these resources: *www.zondervan.com*.
7. *www.shorelinechurch.org/c/weeklyreading/*.
8. See note 1.

Chapter 7: *High Expectations*
1. Luke 9:22–24
2. Matthew 22:36–38
3. I love Gary Thomas's book *Sacred Pathways*. It looks at the various ways believers grow in faith and connect with God. Also, the team at the Willow Creek Association (WCA) continues to develop its *Reveal* resources and is shaping

them into an online tool to help churches and believers focus more intentionally on personal spiritual growth. You can learn more about this on the WCA Web site: *www.willowcreek.com/*.

4. John 13:1–17
5. See endnote 2, from chapter 6.
6. Matthew 5:13–14
7. 1 Peter 3:15
8. See notes for additional resources on this topic in note 1 for chapter 10.
9. This is addressed in greater detail in chapter 10.
10. See notes for additional resources on this topic in the endnotes of chapter 10, note 1.
11. Matthew 6:21
12. Malachi 1:6–18

Chapter 8: *Tough Skin and Soft Hearts*
1. This great book would be a helpful read for any church leader. It was published by Bethany House in 1994.
2. Hebrews 12:2
3. 2 Corinthians 11:24
4. 2 Timothy 3:12

Chapter 9: *Taking Holy Risks*
1. Acts 4; 2 Corinthians 3:12; Hebrews 10:38–39
2. Genesis 12:1–4
3. John Calvin, *Instruction in Faith (1537)* (Louisville, KY: The Westminster Press, 1977).
4. Calvin's commentary on Genesis 18:25

Chapter 10: *Looking Out*
1. These books are titled: *Organic Outreach for Ordinary People* (this is about personal evangelism); *Organic Outreach for Ordinary Churches* (this is about shifting the culture of a local church to be outward and evangelistic); and *Organic Outreach for Ordinary Families*, which I wrote with my wife, Sherry. All three books are published by Zondervan.
2. Matthew 5:13–15
3. 1 Peter 3:15
4. Matthew 28:19–20
5. Luke 15:3–5
6. I have used *Becoming a Contagious Christian* and *Just Walk Across the Room* by Bill Hybels, and I have developed the Organic Outreach curriculum.

7. Published by Zondervan in 1999, this is a great book for a church that wants to maintain integrity in worship but be sensitive to spiritual seekers.
8. Calvin: *Institutes of the Christian Religion,* 4.1.7

Chapter 11: *The "Wow" Factor*

1. George Barna, *Transforming Children into Spiritual Champions* (Ventura, CA: Regal Books, 2003), 18.
2. Sue Miller, "A New Day," *Willow* Magazine, Issue 3, 2005.
3. Haggai 1:4, 8
4. 1 Corinthians 10:31
5. Used with permission.
6. 1 Corinthians 1:27

Chapter 12: *U-Turn Myths*

1. For more information, please visit *www.dailymedbible.org.*
2. 1 Timothy 4:16

Chapter 13: *You-Turns: From You-Turn to U-Turn*

1. Used with permission.
2. Psalm 105:1
3. Used with permission.

Bob Bouwer (MDiv, Western Theological Seminary) has been leading Faith Church in South Holland, Illinois, and Dyer, Indiana, through a U-Turn experience from 1990 to the present. Bouwer is founder and executive director of U-Turn Church Ministries Inc., which holds conferences to help congregations and denominations move toward health and growth. He speaks nationally and provides resources for churches and leaders on how to effectively walk through a turnaround process. He is also the visionary leader of The Ravines in Lowell, Indiana, a marriage hospital that creates U-Turn experiences for marriages that need to find a hope-filled way forward. He lives in Indiana.

Kevin G. Harney (MDiv, Fuller Seminary; DMin, Western Theological Seminary) led Corinth Reformed Church in Byron Center, Michigan, through a U-Turn experience from 1993–2006. He is currently senior pastor of Shoreline Community Church in Monterey, California. Harney is the author of *Organic Outreach for Ordinary People, Leadership from the Inside Out, Seismic Shifts, Finding a Church You Can Love,* and more than sixty small-group guides, as well as curriculum and numerous articles. He also does extensive teaching and speaking both nationally and internationally. He lives in California.